The Indians of Yoknapatawpha

The Indians of Yoknapatawpha

A Study in Literature and History

LEWIS M. DABNEY

LOUISIANA STATE UNIVERSITY PRESS/BATON ROUGE

ISBN 0-0871-0058-7
Library of Congress Catalog Card Number 73–77659
Copyright © 1974 by Louisiana State University Press
All rights reserved
Manufactured in the United States of America
Printed by The TJM Corporation, Baton Rouge, Louisiana
Designed by Albert Crochet

Acknowledgment is made to Mrs. Jill Faulkner Summers and to the Alderman Library, University of Virginia, for permission to quote from the manuscripts of "A Justice" and "Red Leaves" and from the typescript of "The Old People."

Acknowledgment is also made to Random House, Inc., for permission to quote from the following copyrighted works of William Faulkner: *Go Down, Moses* and *Collected Stories of William Faulkner.*

To the Memory of Edmund Wilson

"Though gravediggers' toil be long,
   Sharp their spades, their muscles strong,
   They but thrust their buried men
   Back in the human mind again."

Contents

Acknowledgments   ix

I   The Indians of Yoknapatawpha   3

II   The Roots of Faulkner's Legend   19

III   "Lo!"   43

IV   "A Courtship"   57

V   "A Justice"   72

VI   "Red Leaves"   90

VII   Sam Fathers and *Go Down, Moses*   118

Index   159

✍ Acknowledgments

I am grateful to all who have helped during the writing of this book. Philip Allen, M. E. Bradford, Calvin S. Brown, Malcolm Cowley, Murray C. Falkner, and Robert Farris Thompson provided information or advice. Peter Irvine, Philip Allen, and George Szanto offered useful criticism of the manuscript, and Linda Griggs helped make the index. Mrs. Jill Faulkner Summers and Random House granted permission to quote from Faulkner's writing. Cleanth Brooks, Daniel Aaron, and Susan Turner have been generous in their interest in the work. Sarah Dabney, to whom I always owe most, was its judicious critic from the beginning.

The Indians of Yoknapatawpha

I ❧ The Indians of Yoknapatawpha

The Indians are the neglected people in Faulkner. They are the first phase of his Yoknapatawpha legend, the point of departure of his novels, and they have even been called his most successful creations, yet their world has never been explored.[1] Faulkner wrote four stories of the Mississippi Chickasaws and Choctaws in the time when settlers and their black slaves were coming in along the old southern frontier, before the forced migration of the southern tribes in the 1830s. "A Courtship," "A Justice," "Red Leaves," and "Lo!" make up the section of the *Collected Stories* called "The Wilderness."[2] The Indians in these stories are unmistakably Faulkner characters, humorous, grim, governed by fate, stereotyped on occasion, but never patronized. Tall tales with a base in history and folklore, the stories form a loose chronicle of

1. For the praise of Faulkner's Chickasaws, see Miller MacLure, "William Faulkner," *Queen's Quarterly*, LXXII (Autumn, 1956), 336–37, reprinted in Francis Lee Utley, Lynn Z. Bloom, and Arthur F. Kinney (eds.), *Bear, Man, and God: Seven Approaches to William Faulkner's "The Bear"* (New York, 1964), 165.
2. *Collected Stories of William Faulkner* (New York, 1950), 313–403. Quotations from the Indian stories are from this volume. Page references will be omitted.

Indian responses to white men and black, an alternately intense and amusing background for Faulkner's America and our own.

"A Justice" introduces Sam Fathers, who tells of his mixed racial origins. Readers know Sam Fathers as Faulkner's noble savage and Vanishing American in the epic, elegiac, to some extent redemptive hunting ritual of "The Bear." The four stories lead into the Indian legend of "The Bear" and *Go Down, Moses*, which absorbs both black and white culture and is passed on through Sam Fathers to Isaac McCaslin. The ritual greeting of "Oleh, Grandfather" is taken over from "Red Leaves." Spoken to the great stag which Sam shows the boy, and to the snake Ike later sees at Sam's grave, it brings into focus the American mythology of manhood in nature, of the lost purity of the wilderness. Faulkner reaches back to older cosmologies preceding all society, history, ownership.

He is, in fact, the one fiction writer of consequence since before the Civil War to make substantial use of the Indian subject. "The Bear" is not the only classic that resulted. "The Old People," which establishes Sam Fathers in the hunt, stands with Faulkner's finest work, as do "Red Leaves" and "A Justice"—the one a cruel fable of life and death, of what men can inflict and endure, the other an exuberant fusion of humor and saga. In both, the Indians hold black slaves, as the Mississippi tribes did in this period. "Lo!" and "A Courtship," lighter tales of Indians and whites, similarly revise the redskin myth. The first turns an appeal to the Great White Father into a sit-in at the White House, the second celebrates the brotherhood of the male sex.

"The Bear" aside, these stories account for a handful of items in the huge Faulkner bibliography.[3] "Red Leaves" is famous but has never received a close reading; "A Justice"—which opens Cowley's Viking *Portable Faulkner*—has been largely ignored. The obscurity of "A Courtship" and "Lo!" is easier to explain. Individually they amount to less, and they can be found only in the *Collected Stories*, anomalous among stories of World War I, the twenties, small-town life. Criticism reached this volume last; the four Indian tales do not appear here in their order as a chronicle, nor were they written in such order.[4] There are other factors in the neglect of Faulkner's Indians. The glimpses of the Chickasaws in *Requiem for a Nun* gave no hint of the world behind them, and the reaction against Cowley's idea of the Yoknapatawpha saga discouraged curiosity. Even in the apogee of "The Bear," in the 1950s and early 1960s, Sam Fathers' roots and significance were unexplored.

The obscurity of Faulkner's historical basis is the central cause: few know much about this phase of southern Indian history. It was not always so. In the early nineteenth century the Cherokee, Chickasaw, Choctaw,

3. Maurice Beebe, "Criticism of William Faulkner: A Selected Checklist," *Modern Fiction Studies*, XIII (Spring, 1967), 115–61, includes only half a dozen books and articles touching on the Indian stories. There have since been an essay on the four tales, individual studies of "A Courtship" and "Red Leaves," and a note on "A Justice," all by Elmo Howell. M. E. Bradford is the author of essays on "Lo!" and "A Justice" and a forthcoming note on the Indian idea of property in relation to "The Bear," the substance of which he has kindly allowed me to use.

4. In the *Collected Stories*, "Red Leaves" is first, followed by "A Justice" and "A Courtship," with "Lo!" last. This is the reverse of their order as a chronicle. It is the order in which they were originally published in magazines, except that "Lo!" has changed places with "A Courtship" to keep the tales of Ikkemotubbe's tribe together. "The order of the Indian stories was set by the author," according to Albert Erskine of Random House, in a letter to the author, January 20, 1971.

Creek, and Seminole nations were widely known as the Five Civilized Tribes, in tribute to their adaptation to peace and the white man's ways. Indigenous peoples, more numerous and less primitive than the northern tribes, they had retained a relatively homogeneous block of territory from the Carolinas to the Mississippi River through the long Anglo-French wars and the Revolution. Under American rule they became part-time farmers and artisans or opened up plantations on the tribal lands. Some sent their children to missionary schools. They did not abandon their own culture—Sequoyah's invention of a written language for the Cherokees is still famous. A true American pluralism seemed briefly possible.[5]

This was due to the historical accident that the United States was then a seaboard country. A federal government run by gentlemen stood between the Indians and the land hunger which was building behind the frontier. But the westerner Andrew Jackson betrayed his Indian allies after the Creek War of 1813, dictating a cession which opened a wide corridor to white settlement from the Tennessee to the Gulf of Mexico, and beginning to press all the southern tribes to move across the Mississippi. They held out through the 1820s, a period of relative harmony on the frontier, but when Jackson became president— "a Great White Father with a sword," as Faulkner says— he forced them to trade their homelands for tracts in the Indian Territory. The protests of the Indians, supported

5. See especially R. S. Cotterill, *The Southern Indians: The Story of the Civilized Tribes Before Removal* (Norman, Okla., 1954), a diplomatic and political history, and Dale Van Every, *Disinherited: The Lost Birthright of the American Indian* (New York, 1966), which gives a social history as well. Van Every emphasizes the experience of the Cherokees, whose extraordinary progress in one generation, culminating in their legal struggle to hold onto their lands, made their expulsion to the wild western land the more a mockery.

by men from Davy Crockett to Daniel Webster, were useless, and the westward journey, observed by Tocqueville among others, became known as the Trail of Tears. While a third of the Choctaws chose to remain on small reservations in central Mississippi, the removal of the Chickasaws was complete. There were no Indians in Faulkner's part of the state in his lifetime.[6]

The Chickasaws, Choctaws, and Cherokees were the aristocrats of the region after the destruction of the Natchez by the French. As late as the 1820s the Chickasaws are said to have ranked with the greatest warriors and hunters of the North American Indians.[7] A small nation, whose population varied between thirty-five hundred and forty-five hundred, they controlled what became western Kentucky and Tennessee as well as northern Mississippi. Lafayette County was their territory, and Chickasaws signed the old land deeds that so stimulated Faulkner's imagination. The lands of their twenty thousand Choctaw cousins extended south to the Gulf. Choctaws were farmers and traders as well as great defensive fighters; as hunters they were expert at coming upon an animal with-

6. Jackson's personality and politics are pungently evoked in the appendix of William Faulkner, *The Sound and the Fury* (New York, n. d.), 3. Like Ikkemotubbe, he is seen as a progenitor of the Compson line. On the protests and removal, see Van Every, *Disinherited*. See also Grant Foreman, *Indian Removal: The Emigration of the Five Civilized Tribes* (Norman, Okla. 1953), and Arthur H. DeRosier, Jr., *The Removal of the Choctaw Indians* (New York, 1970). The Trail of Tears was a phrase first applied to the route of the Cherokees from their Appalachian Mountain country to Indian Territory in 1838. The Choctaws and Creeks had already made the journey. Tocqueville chanced to see and commemorated the Choctaw crossing of the Mississippi on a harsh December day in 1831. It was an occasion for tears, but what most impressed him was the Indians' absolute silence. Alexis de Tocqueville, *Democracy in America* (New York, 1954), I, 352–53.

7. Horatio B. Cushman, *History of the Choctaw-Chickasaw and Natchez Indians* (Greenville, Tex., 1899), 527. For Choctaw hunting practices, see p. 180.

out being seen. The languages of the nations are similar, and their material and spiritual cultures were in many ways alike. Both met white men halfway, resisting governments and settlers but remaining hospitable to the French and Scottish traders and trappers, who intermarried with them and, by the late eighteenth century, had produced a mixed-blood class of leaders. The mixtures of Indian and white names in Faulkner's tales reflect this development.[8]

They also absorbed the white man's slaves, by accepting them as runaways and by purchasing them. That southern Indians held blacks as slaves, before and after the Indians' removal to the West—the major tribes fought with the Confederacy in the Civil War—is almost forgotten today. There were Negro slaves among the Chickasaws as early as 1747, according to the British trader James Adair.[9] They acted as interpreters between their masters and the whites. They were acquired as personal servants—prestige items—as well as to work the land. Enslavement of Indian by Indian had time limits and was not hereditary, although the ancient Chickasaws maimed their slaves so that they could not flee. The forms of Negro slavery varied, but the institution expanded as Indian agriculture developed. "The Five Civilized Tribes," historian Kenneth Porter writes, "became large slaveholders for the same reason as their white neighbors, while the more northerly tribes abstained for the same sort of rea-

8. The standard work on the Choctaws is Angie Debo, *The Rise and Fall of the Choctaw Republic* (Norman, Okla. 1934). Arrell M. Gibson, *The Chickasaws* (Norman, Okla., 1971), reflects the later scholarship on the southern tribes. None of the histories affords much sense of what the daily life of the Indians was like in the early period of assimilation, but Gibson treats the years before removal in detail.

9. James Adair, *History of the American Indians*, ed. S. C. Williams (Johnson City, Tenn., 1930), 441.

son." [10] Most owners were of mixed Indian and white blood. "Among the full bloods slaves exercized many privileges," another writer says, "and in many instances their condition of servitude was hardly discernible, while among the mixed bloods they were required to be slaves indeed in all manner of work." [11] But the tribes seldom matched the intensive market agriculture of the white plantation. The numbers of runaways along the frontier testify to the appeal of Indians as masters. It has also been suggested, that slaves were attracted by the opportunity to have a role in the highly structured Indian societies.[12]

The nations, however, were divided in their social policies. The Creeks and the small band of Seminoles were the more egalitarian, and they eventually absorbed their slave populations by intermarriage. The Seminoles would also allow the blacks to live as separate tribes and cultivate their own land, more like vassals than chattel slaves. On the other hand the Cherokees, Chickasaws, and Choctaws developed a caste society and "were insistent on racial purity." They passed laws forbidding intermarriage with Negro slaves, regulating the blacks' property rights, and denying them their rights as citizens. There were exceptions in practice, as novelist R. A.

10. Kenneth W. Porter, "Relations Between Negroes and Indians Within the Present Limits of the United States," *Journal of Negro History*, XVII (July, 1932), 321. Porter, however, also notes that the forms of slavery varied among the different tribes and with individual members of the same tribe. For the view of a proslavery white southerner, see "Slavery Among the Indians" (signed 'C'), *Southern Literary Messenger*, XXVIII (May, 1859), 333.

11. Wyatt F. Jeltz, "The Relations of Negroes and Choctaw and Chickasaw Indians," *Journal of Negro History*, XXXIII (January, 1948), 26.

12. Peter Farb, *Man's Rise to Civilization* (New York, 1968), 316. Farb sees the escaped black as running from a state of nonidentity among the whites: "He chose to be a slave under Indian masters because they gave him something that the Whites denied him: the opportunity to exist, even as a chattel, inside a rigid social structure."

Lafferty avers by making one of his Choctaw hero's three wives a black. As the Creeks and Seminoles became Africanized the positions of the other tribes hardened.[13]

Faulkner treats the Indians as slaveholders in order to gain perspective on his own culture. Although his subject is the Mississippi tribes, he allows for the fraternization from which Sam Fathers derives. In "A Justice" black man and Indian are sexual rivals with no race prejudice on either side, and the chief protects the black family. The People and the black people work together under his eagle eye. In "Red Leaves," by contrast, the Chickasaws look down on their slaves and have gone into the slave trade, as Gunnar Myrdal notes that some tribes did.[14] Faulkner imagines the survival of the archaic within the southern scene. Working from a grim local tale, he stages the Indians' pursuit and recapture of their dead chief's slave, who must be buried along with his master.

Faulkner once spoke of having made up his Indians, and the imaginative freedom of the stories obscures their

13. On the Seminoles, see Porter, "Relations Between Negroes and Indians," 323–50; also Porter, "The Negro Abraham," *Florida Historical Quarterly*, XXV (July, 1946), an account of a black leader of the tribe, and "The Episode of Osceola's Wife," *Florida Historical Quarterly*, XXVI (July, 1947), a refutation of the legend of her Negro blood. Jeltz, "Relations of Negroes and Choctaw and Chickasaw Indians," 30, describes the Chickasaw and Choctaw legislation on racial purity. For information on the Cherokees, see Van Every, *Disinherited*, 81–82. R. A. Lafferty, *Okla Hannali* (New York, 1972), 13, calls the enslavement of blacks among the Choctaws comparable to that of Indian by Indian. But a traveler in the Indian Territory in the 1840s was impressed that the Choctaws, while fond of ceremonies and especially funerals, buried their slaves without services of any kind. "Mr. C., the carpenter, expressed deep sympathy for Mrs. R. in the loss of so valuable a piece of property. 'Cato,' said he, 'was a valuable and good boy, well worth six hundred dollars. Mrs. R. is very unfortunate in losing such a slave!' " Henry C. Benson, *Life Among the Choctaw Indians, and Sketches of the South-West* (Cincinatti, 1860; reprinted, New York, 1970), 295–96.

14. Gunnar Myrdal, *An American Dilemma* (New York, 1962), 124.

relation to history.[15] All are tall tales, and his taste for
the bizarre is accentuated by the remoteness of the scene.
They are funny, from the slapstick sit-in at the White
House in "Lo!" to the bitter comedy of the Chickasaws
in "Red Leaves," who spout the rhetoric of the white
man's burden while hunting the slave to his death. The
Gothic strain here and in "A Justice" looks back to Poe
and Brockden Brown; the romanticism of "A Courtship," like that of "The Bear," recalls Cooper and Melville. Faulkner's Indians, however, are neither nature's
noblemen nor brutes, the conventional alternatives of
the nineteenth century.[16] His exotic detail and his mono-
syllabic, darkly comical Indian speech, which owes something to Hemingway's dialogue, make the tales unique.
Elmo Howell, their first serious critic, sees them as an
extravagant creation *ex nihilo*:

> A deserted steamboat drawn on cypress logs twelve miles
> through the woods to become the dwelling of a chief, with
> the chief himself sitting on deck with a slave boy behind
> him to drive away "the flying beasts"; the ceremonial of
> a chief's burial, along with his dog, his horse, and his slave,
> who are slaughtered beside an open grave, followed by a

15. Professor Calvin S. Brown, of the University of Georgia, who comes
from Oxford and knew Faulkner in his youth, writes as follows: "My
mother (whose grandmother grew up in Oxford, and who was a local
historian herself) once asked him where he got his Indians from, since
she knew of no real sources, and he answered matter-of-factly, 'Mrs.
Brown, I made them up.' " Calvin S. Brown to the author, October 28,
1971.

16. In *The Savages of America: A Study of the Indian and the Idea of
Civilization* (Baltimore, 1953), Roy Harvey Pearce explores the ambivalence of early American literature toward the Indian. Juxtaposing the
noble savage of drama and poetry with the bloodily ignoble savage of
the captivity narratives, he shows how an either-or convention was
gradually subsumed in a larger idea of the remoteness of the Indian
world from the white man's standards. This is Faulkner's starting point,
but he does not allow the reader to think his own civilization superior.

feast of baked dog and succotash; the medicine man who burns sticks in a skunk vest; the young men with their game cocks in wicker hampers; the litter and filth and careless abandon of savage life; treachery and sudden death—this strange world, caught in a lurid light against the darkness of a forest, has a way of imposing its own validity.[17]

"With no experience to draw upon and with his aversion to research," Howell writes, "Faulkner makes no pretension to accuracy in his treatment of Indian life." But Indians ate dog, invented succotash, went in for cockfighting, and Choctaws in Mississippi are still weaving baskets. Faulkner knew that the steamboat episode in "A Justice" was possible—that the tribes were impressed by steamboats, which were sometimes wrecked and abandoned, that "at this time," as he wrote to Cowley during the making of the Viking *Portable*, "the Tallahatchie, running from the Chickasaw across the Choctaw nation, was navigable; steamboats came up it." Both nations had buried horses with their chiefs; and in an Oxford woman's account of the town in 1936 one finds a tale of local Chickasaws who were prevented from sending a slave to join his master in the other world.[18] Faulkner is "sublimating the actual into the apocryphal," as he once defined his method.[19] The Chickasaws and Choctaws, he wrote, "were slightly different people in behavior. The

17. Elmo Howell, "William Faulkner and the Mississippi Indians," *Georgia Review*, XXI (Fall, 1967), 386–87.
18. Minnie Smith Holt, "Oxford, Mississippi" (Typescript, University of Mississippi Library, 1936), 25. This passage in Mrs. Holt's valuable record of the local lore is cited by Ward L. Miner, *The World of William Faulkner* (New York, 1952), 22, who fails, however, to connect it with "Red Leaves."
19. "Interview with Jean Stein vanden Heuvel," in James B. Meriwether and Michael Millgate (eds.), *Lion in the Garden: Interviews with William Faulkner, 1926–1962* (New York, 1968), 255.

line dividing the two nations passed near my home [Oxford]. I merely moved a tribe slightly at need. . . . 'Red Leaves' actually were Chickasaws." [20]

His chronicle reverses the nineteenth-century view of the Indians' progress. "Lo!" (1934) looks back to their first confrontations with the settlers and with Washington power. In Washington the red men more than hold their own; in making the Great White Father a chief they seem to have the strength even to assimilate the whites. "A Courtship" (1948, written about 1943) is Faulkner's version of the brotherhood of Indian and frontiersman in the days of Davy Crockett and Sam Houston. The young Ikkemotubbe of "A Courtship" becomes Doom, "the Man" or chief, in "A Justice" (1931), and is remembered in "Red Leaves" (1930), stories about the same tribe, which is first Choctaw, then Chickasaw. The Basket family is another source of continuity here; it provides the girl of "A Courtship," the narrator of "A Justice," and one of the tribal spokesmen in "Red Leaves." "Red Leaves" recapitulates the tribal history. Faulkner is creating a vanished world, not moralizing with Isaac McCaslin, but he takes the Indians into a decay that parallels the growth of plantation slavery.

He wrote the last tale first, and their sequence remains a loose one, in the spirit of folk history. "Lo!" is early in feeling, yet the president is partly drawn from Andrew Jackson; "Red Leaves" evokes both the decadence of the Indians and their primeval past. "A Courtship," along with *Go Down, Moses* and *Requiem for a Nun*, follows a different genealogy from "Red Leaves" and "A Justice."

20. Faulkner to Malcolm Cowley, August 16, 1945, in Malcolm Cowley, *The Faulkner-Cowley File: Letters and Memories, 1944–1962* (New York, 1966), 25–27.

"I never made a genealogical or chronological chart," he told Cowley, "perhaps because I knew I would take liberties with both—which I have." [21] There are practical reasons for this. His material comes from the period between the establishment of a trading post and U.S. agency in the Mississippi Territory, just before 1800, and the removal of the Indians in the 1830s. One generation's experience is expanded into two or three generations, to do justice to its varied possibilities.[22]

The difference between the stories with whites and those with blacks is the decisive one. The encounter and partial assimilation of red and white men do not engage him deeply. "Lo!" and "A Courtship" are a master's minor work, relaxed in tone. Serious themes are developed as entertainments. In "A Justice" and "Red Leaves" the Indian subject meets the Mississippi Faulkner knew. Slavery gives him urgency, and the presence of the blacks makes the Indian stage more real. The meeting of the red and the black is dramatized in Sam

21. Faulkner to Malcolm Cowley, *Faulkner-Cowley File*, 55. In "A Justice" and "Red Leaves" Doom's father is appropriately nameless, while Doom is Issetibbeha's father and Moketubbe's grandfather. But in *Go Down, Moses* Doom becomes Issetibbeha's son and Moketubbe's cousin. The dynastic history here excludes the action of "Red Leaves." There is also a contradiction between "Red Leaves" and "A Justice," published within a few months of each other. Herman Basket in "A Justice" is apparently the son of Three Basket in "Red Leaves," although the latter story recapitulates the tribal history.

22. In *Requiem for a Nun* the trading post is established before 1800, thirty years before Jefferson gets its name. The first white settlers begin to arrive a few years later, although in *The Reivers* Faulkner has the first plantation owner, Grenier, arriving in the 1790s. Mississippi became a state in 1817. Lafayette was one of the ten counties created from the Chickasaw Cession in the Treaty of Pontotoc in 1832. For this and other background information see Elizabeth M. Kerr, *Yoknapatawpha: Faulkner's "Little Postage Stamp of Native Soil"* (New York, 1969), 79–84, especially the footnotes.

Fathers, a far more powerful figure than Boon Hogganbeck with his mixed Indian and white blood.

Through Sam Fathers the chronicle leads into *Go
Down, Moses*. In the novel, as in "A Justice," he is the old
"Negro" carpenter and blacksmith at the boy's (Quentin
Compson, then Isaac McCaslin) grandfather's farm, who
tells stories of his Indian forebears. The Indian theme is
used to dignify the man of color, and his black social
identity is underscored. He is the "son of a negro slave
. . . in the battered and faded overalls and the frayed five-
cent straw hat which had been the badge of the negro's
slavery and was now the regalia of his freedom." When
he says to McCaslin, "Let me go," and then, "I'm going
now," the quest for freedom in the spiritual "Go Down,
Moses" is implicit.

Where Sam Fathers wants to go is the wilderness;
there he is "the Indian," respected for his woodsman's
skill and profound understanding of the woods, preser-
ver of the tradition the tribe abandoned for the white
man's ways. The Indians of "A Justice" are unromantic,
but in the novel their black offspring becomes a Chickasaw prince, at one point "the old dark man sired on *both*
sides by savage kings" (italics added). The noble savage
is adapted to the southern scene and to the racial guilts of
Faulkner's time as opposed to those of nineteenth-century
Americans.

Doom's character too is changed in *Go Down, Moses*.
The archetypal young male of "A Courtship," the Machi-
avellian despot of "A Justice," an enlightened one where
the blacks are concerned, becomes a shadowy agent of the
larger southern destiny. He is the man who sold the tribal
domain, "knowing better." Faulkner was impressed by

the idea of the primitive communism of the Indians and by the description, in Rousseau's *Discourse on Inequality,* of how man falls away from such a state of grace.[23] Doom also sells his black son to a white neighbor, anticipating all the comparable acts of repudiation in Yoknapatawpha. If "The Bear" is a Mississippi *Paradise Lost,* the chief is Faulkner's Adam, and the slaveholding of the Indians helps Ike McCaslin justify the ways of God to man.

A skeptic could say Faulkner makes the Indians scapegoats for the white man's sins while rationalizing the expulsion of the tribes. His Indians are never so historical as to be pure victims. His whites, however, fail God most of all, bringing upon themselves the Civil War. In "The Bear" he is drawn toward a mythology in which, by endurance and fortitude, the blacks are destined to inherit the earth, after red man and white have failed to destroy it. Meanwhile the hunting ritual is an expression of natural piety and a release from society's corruption. "Sam Fathers set me free," Ike says. Both men are confirmed as Indians through their greeting of the totem animal who represents the doom and immortality of the wilderness.

To the ethnologist, as to the sober citizen, this may be pure romance, but the larger themes of "The Old People" and "The Bear" are clearly historical. Faulkner echoes great Indian spokesmen of the past who affirmed man's unity with the land, in life and death, and who rejected the possibility of individual ownership or sale of land. So too is his lament for a culture which, holding these truths self-evident, saw its world intruded upon, its

23. Jean Jacques Rousseau, "Discourse on the Origins and Foundations of Inequality Among Men," *The First and Second Discourses,* ed. Roger O. Masters (New York, 1964), 141–42.

hunting range destroyed, its leaders isolated and convinced of the doom of the tribe. Chief Joseph, who loved
freedom, melancholy Seattle and Cochise, Black Elk himself, who in his old age held to the magnificent unavailing
vision of his youth, are the ancestors of Sam Fathers and
Isaac McCaslin.[24] Through the pride of the South, its
piety, and resistance to assimilation, Faulkner responds
to the hunt and the Indian legend.

The Chickasaws and Choctaws of the four stories are
in a different sense historical. They may seem caricatures
or whites in disguise, but they plot the curve and show the
paradoxes of assimilation in this dark corner of the past.
Its obscurity is an asset to Faulkner, for he is free to ex-
ploit the tall tale and the traditions of oral narrative and
American humor. One can scarcely object to this in the
name of the Indians, well known for their tall tales. Vine
Deloria stresses his people's love of humor, and in the
American Indian Reader Jeannette Henry says that
"when the art of story-telling dies, we Natives too will

24. See Chief Joseph, "An Indian's Views of Indian Affairs," Seattle,
"The White Man Will Never Be Alone," and Cochise, "Why Has the
Virgin Mary Never Entered the Wigwam of the Apache?" in Thomas E.
Sanders and Walter W. Peek (eds.), *Literature of the American Indian*
(New York and Beverly Hills, 1973), 295–310, 282–85, 291–92. See also
W. C. Wanderwerth, *Indian Oratory: Famous Speeches by Noted Indian
Chieftains* (Norman, Okla., 1971). Kiowa Chief Satanta's speech on 179–
80 would have had a strong appeal in the post–Civil War South: "A long
time ago," he concludes, "this land belonged to our fathers; but when I
go up to the river I see camps of soldiers on its banks. These soldiers cut
down my timber; they kill my buffalo; and when I see that, my heart feels
like bursting; I feel sorry. I have spoken." At the conclusion of *Black Elk
Speaks*, as told through John G. Neihardt (Lincoln, Nebr., 1961) there are
several passages suggestive of the old Ike of "Delta Autumn": "It is hard
to follow one great vision in this world of darkness and of many changing
shadows," he says (254); "And I, to whom so great a vision was given in
my youth,—you see me now a pitiful old man who has done nothing, for
the nation's hoop is broken and scattered. There is no center any longer,
and the sacred tree is dead" (276). The work was first published in 1932,
when Faulkner had just begun the Indian stories.

die. It is our favorite sport, our best means of communica-
tion, our one remaining evidence of a joyful spirit. . . .
It is practically impossible to reconstruct the nature of
Indian story-telling," she concedes.[25] Faulkner's version
is the Sam Fathers at whose feet Quentin and Isaac sit.
Solemnly described in "The Old People," in "A Justice"
Sam develops serious themes as entertainment, just as
Faulkner does in the related tales.

For a writer with Faulkner's creative powers, the Indians were a usable past in Henry James's sense. They
were the past of a land preoccupied with the past, where
the white man's tenure was but a century old. Dispossessed by a more "advanced" civilization, they shared this
with both the white South and the black, and had mingled their blood with both. His interest in conflicts of
blood mixture drew Faulkner to the Indian subject, as
did the difficulties involved in seeing the blacks clearly.
Behind him was a tradition going back through Jefferson
to William Byrd, a southern respect for Indians which co-
existed with condescension to blacks until Faulkner's
own work.[26] The larger American milieu and mythology
are also implicit, Faulkner's literary and local sources are
easier to detect than usual. The artist is sovereign, and he
is a voice of the land itself, emerging from the fragments
of a vanishing history and of a folk culture.

25. Jeannette Henry (ed.), *The American Indian Reader: Literature*
(San Francisco, 1973), 60.

26. In "Notes on Virginia," Adrienne Koch and William Peden (eds.),
The Life and Selected Writings of Thomas Jefferson (New York, 1944),
compare 210–13, on the American Indians, and 256–62, on the blacks.
Jefferson rationalizes the limitations of the Indians and refutes their
European detractors, while piling up empirical evidence of the inequality of blacks with whites. Byrd admired the Indians sufficiently to suggest
that whites intermarry with them in return for portions of their land.

II ✌ The Roots of Faulkner's Legend

I

Like Hawthorne's Puritans, Faulkner's Indians go back to a man's responses to the remains of the past. Faulkner's own people, in Mississippi a scant three generations, had left no trophies so ancient as the scarlet letter or the house of the seven gables. But the Indian mounds in the state appear as settings in his fiction. There are several around Oxford, and he owned a book on the archaeology of Mississippi, with pictures of the great mounds to the south. In his article on Mississippi the bones and artifacts from the mounds are reminders of the white man's predecessors in the land. An excavation party of white people anticipates Lucas Beauchamp's treasure hunt in "The Fire and the Hearth." If one can scarcely imagine Faulkner excavating a mound to complete the anatomy of his land, as Jefferson did, he is not far from Hawthorne when with Lucas he uncovers the single coin, gift of "the old earth . . . the old ancestors." [1]

In "A Bear Hunt," a story of a practical joke involv-

1. William Faulkner, *Go Down, Moses* (New York, 1942), 38. Quotations from "The Old People" and "The Bear" are also from this edition of the novel, and future page references will be omitted. The book on the Indians is Calvin S. Brown, *Archaeology of Mississippi* (University, Miss., 1926), by the father of the Calvin S. Brown to whom I am indebted for information about the background of the Indian stories. See also "Mississippi," in James B. Meriwether (ed.), *Essays, Speeches, and Public Letters by William Faulkner* (New York, 1965), 12–13.

ing some Indians whom Faulkner invented for the occasion, the narrator digresses on his boyhood impression of a mound rising all by itself "in the wild, flat jungle of river bottom." It was, he says, "as though the yells and hatchets we associated with Indians through the hidden and secret dime novels which we passed among ourselves were but trivial and momentary manifestations of what dark power still dwelled or lurked there, sinister, a little sardonic. . . ." He may, of course, have gone on from dime novels to Gothic romances. He speaks of a remnant of Chickasaws living near the mound, who seemed its guardians. These are the Indians of "A Bear Hunt." [2] He also evokes the sobering experience of camping out on the mound at the age of fifteen. The description of the two boys sitting silently through the night, not making a fire or getting into their blankets, just waiting for the light to come, reads like a memory.

Calvin S. Brown, a scholar who grew up in Oxford a few years after Faulkner, speaks of knowing the mounds and collecting arrowheads, but stresses the remoteness of the Indian past, as against the vivid Civil War legends.[3] In "A Bear Hunt" Faulkner's imagination joins the two. He calls the mound "as much a part of our lives and back-

2. It is interesting that Robert Silverberg, in *Mound Builders of Ancient America* (Greenwich, Conn., 1968), 326–27, attributes to the southern tribes this sort of relationship to the mound builders. "They lived about the old temple mounds," keeping up the customs while their way of life became a very different one, until they "could no longer remember that it was their own great-grandfathers who had built the mounds." Faulkner grasped something of the continuity and change of the Indian culture of his region.

3. "The Civil War was very much alive in local oral tradition, but not the Chickasaws. Our knowledge of them was essentially like our knowledge of the Incas and the Pharaohs, though perhaps a bit more real because of the arrowheads." Calvin S. Brown to the author, October 28, 1971.

ground as the land itself, as the lost Civil War and Sherman's march, or that there were Negroes among us living in economic competition who bore our family names; only more immediate, more potential and alive." One sees how the dual heritage of southern defeat and Negro slavery gave the Indians a power for him they have not had for other modern American writers. They were the first dispossessed and ravaged people of the South. "I think the ghost of that ravishment lingers in the land," he said in 1957, "that the land is inimical to the white man because of the unjust way in which it was taken from Ikkemotubbe and his people." [4] The Gothic is adapted to social criticism.

Leslie Fiedler asserts that "the image of the Vanishing American has haunted all Americans." [5] If so Faulkner speaks for us all in his image of Doom in the appendix of *The Sound and the Fury*, a "dispossessed American king" who is progenitor of the Compson line; of Queen Mohataha of *Requiem for a Nun*, who makes her X and turns her wagon west. What haunts him, however, is not the Indians' fate per se, bitter as this was. He does not follow the Trail of Tears to Indian Territory, noting only the irony that descendants of these tribesmen struck oil in the barren land of their exile.[6] The curse on his own land and its relationship to slavery is what he dwells upon, and his true Vanishing Americans are Sam Fathers

4. Frederick Gwynn and Joseph L. Blotner (eds.), *Faulkner in the University: Class Conferences in the University of Virginia, 1957–58* (Charlottesville, Va., 1959), 43.
5. Leslie A. Fiedler, *The Return of the Vanishing American* (New York, 1968), 75.
6. "One day the homeless descendants of the dispossessed would ride supine with drink and splendidly comatose above the dusky allotted harborage of their bones in specially built scarlet-painted hearses and fire-engines." Faulkner, *The Sound and the Fury* (New York, n.d.), 3.

and Isaac McCaslin—Yoknapatawpha is its own kind of melting pot.

The woods and hunting were a happier continuity with Indian times. The frontier heritage which is always Faulkner's answer to the plantation South was very much alive in his boyhood. John Faulkner tells how the boys' mammy, Callie Barr, told stories as she introduced them to the woods; how their father taught his sons to shoot as their turn came, giving them air rifles at eight, .22s at ten, shotguns when they were twelve. On Sunday walks he began their training in wood lore, while talking of hunts he had been on, parts of which tales, John Faulkner says, appear in Faulkner's fiction.[7] He would fox hunt with a friend, Uncle Ike Roberts, sometime sheriff of Lafayette County, and before the boy was in his teens he was following the men on their fox chases. Ike Roberts became one of his own hunting companions when he took up hunting seriously in the 1930s, and the older Isaac McCaslin, "Uncle Ike," is partly modeled on men of this vintage.[8]

Isaac McCaslin's boyhood and his relationship to Sam Fathers go back to Cooper and Melville, to the mythic initiation into nature by the frontiersman or savage. While Faulkner read and praised *Moby-Dick* as an adult, the strong influence of Cooper was part of his boyhood. Murry Falkner remembers "Cooper's tales of the American Indians" as being among their pleasures.[9] What Isaac

7. John Faulkner, *My Brother Bill: An Affectionate Reminiscence* (New York, 1963), 90.

8. See Bramlett Roberts, "A Soft Touch, A Great Heart," in James W. Webb and A. Wigfall Green (eds.), *William Faulkner of Oxford* (Baton Rouge, 1965), 151. See also Jerrold Brite, "A True-Blue Hunter," *ibid.*, 154–61, and John B. Cullen and Floyd Watkins, *Old Times in the Faulkner Country* (Chapel Hill, N. C., 1961).

9. Murry Falkner, *The Falkners of Mississippi* (Baton Rouge, 1967), 17.

McCaslin, Sam Fathers, and Boon Hogganbeck have in common—and Dilsey shares when she says "I've seed de first en de last. . . . I seed de beginnin', en now I sees de endin' "—is the tone of *The Last of the Mohicans*. Boon and Sam are also drawn from individuals—Boon from a man who worked for his father, as Faulkner acknowledged, and Sam, as will shortly be seen, from a storytelling blacksmith at his grandfather's farm outside Oxford. Was he already imagining them in a Cooper scene?

His own initiation did not resemble his hero's. A hunting accident which killed a hound caused him to give up shooting from about the time he was fourteen until he was grown. Its effects on "The Bear" must be taken into account. The accident contributes to the story of Boon and Lion, to the whole theme of the acceptance of death. Meanwhile there were other ways of enjoying the wilderness, "the part of Mississippi that I liked when I was young," Faulkner said at Virginia. Boys played "Indian" games, and one popular sport retained its appeal for him, influencing his sense of the lost Indian world. In his early twenties he was spending Sunday afternoons in elaborate, exhausting contests of hare and hounds with three or four teen-agers in the woods and fields near the University of Mississippi campus. Calvin Brown, who was one of these boys, has shown how Faulkner's manhunts, including the one in "Red Leaves," draw on this experience; and so does the marathon in "A Courtship." [10]

While "The Old People" and "The Bear" combine the hunt and the noble savage with the darker associations of the mounds, the Indians of the stories owe much to popular humor. They emerge from stereotypes as his first im-

10. Calvin S. Brown, "Faulkner's Manhunts: Fact into Fiction," *Georgia Review*, XX (Winter, 1966), 388–95.

ages of the savages derived from dime novels. "O Sister's Son, your eye is a bad eye, like the eye of a bad horse," the then chief says in "A Justice" to young Ikkemotubbe, who will murder him in the manner of Richard III. Faulkner's father always read the brothers the Sunday funnies. The monstrous Moketubbe of "Red Leaves," whose 250 pounds of inert flesh are carried on a litter in pursuit of the doomed slave, is the comic-strip Oriental despot rendered truly malevolent, pathetic, absurd.

Place names in the county reminded one of the Indian past. The tale behind "Red Leaves" was associated with the Toby Tubby Creek northwest of Oxford, *toby* being Chickasaw for old or bent and *tubby* or *tubbe* the word for chief. In the manuscript of the story, Louis Berry is first called *Yo-ko-no-pa-taw-fa*, from the old name for the Yocona River south of town.[11] This is Faulkner's first use of the Chickasaw word, which he translated as *water flowing slow through the flatland.*[12] If there is a Yoknapatawpha saga it begins here.

To flesh out the legend was the natural thing. Faulkner grew up in a world of storytelling, the primary business, Murry Falkner writes, both of their father's livery stable and of stores and offices around the courthouse square, where the customer did not come first.[13] Animals,

11. William Faulkner, untitled manuscript of "Red Leaves" (MS in William Faulkner Collection, Alderman Library, University of Virginia), 1. The division into syllables suggests that he is trying the word on his tongue.

12. "Interviews in Japan," in James B. Meriwether and Michael Millgate (eds.), *Lion in the Garden: Interviews with William Faulkner, 1926–1962* (New York, 1968), 133–34. See also Gwynn and Blotner (eds.), *Faulkner in the University,* 74.

13. "Such commerce as existed was given attention only after it was no longer needed for personal matters," Murry Falkner says. "None there was brash enough to consider that the customer was always right. On the contrary, unless he was both prudent and patient, he was universally

hunting, and fishing were standard subjects there. At home the Falkner boys heard grandmothers and great-aunts telling family stories going back through the Civil War to North Carolina and Scotland, as the Compson dynasty does. Mammy Callie Barr, to whom *Go Down, Moses* is properly dedicated, told of slavery days from her own experiences.

II

In the figure of Sam Fathers, Faulkner represents his debt to folk tradition and ties this to the survival of Indian blood in the land. He presents what, if historical, would be his most important source. There were Choctaws on reservations a hundred miles to the south, descendants of those who had not gone west in the 1830s. In Faulkner's boyhood there were still 1,344 full bloods speaking Choctaw as their mother tongue and keeping up the old customs, including the famous Choctaw ball game.[14] But the local Chickasaws had left only the place

---

judged as being wrong, especially if he dared to interrupt the flow of conversation between the proprietor of the store and his cronies seated about in various comfortable accomodations. The tales they told were on the tall side and were judged not for accuracy but solely on effectiveness of delivery. A man was not even admonished if he told the same tale twice, provided it sounded as good the second time as it did the first." *The Falkners of Mississippi*, 27. Falkner similarly characterizes their father's years of running a livery stable: "It was an easy life and a pleasant one for him, I'm certain. He had his office at the head of the livery stable, a gang of Negroes to attend to the horses, two white men to drive the hacks, and always two to ten cronies to sit about the comfortable stove in his office and tell tall tales about animals, hunting, and fishing, applying themselves to the ever-present crock of good drinking whiskey as the mood and thirst struck them individually and collectively." *Ibid.*, 10. The nostalgic idealization of these passages makes them no less important for an understanding of Faulkner's debt to this storytelling tradition, and of his affirmations of community.

14. This was the number in 1907, according to Angie Debo in *The Rise and Fall of the Choctaw Republic* (Norman, Okla., 1934), 276. See

names and their Xs on the land patents like that to his own property, which he bought in the year he began the Indian stories. There were traces of "the wild blood" in white men and black, lessening during his lifetime. In the appendix to *The Sound and the Fury* in 1945 it is "seen only occasionally in the nose-shape of a Negro on a cotton-wagon or a white sawmill hand or trapper or locomotive fireman." [15]

The scene in the carpenter's shop in "A Justice" (1931) is set before World War I, and Sam Fathers' tale makes him the son of an Indian and a slave woman, named by Doom Had-Two-Fathers. It is repeated with some changes in "The Old People" and is a premise of "The Bear." Behind the Indian master of the hunt, whom Faulkner invented, is another man, "talking about the old days and the People whom he had not had time ever to know and so could not remember (he did not remember ever having seen his father's face), and in place of whom the other race into which his blood had run supplied him with no substitute." Had the writer heard such a mixed blood holding forth on his Indian forbears? Sam Fathers' authenticity has never been explored.

That American Indians and blacks have mingled their blood on a large scale is well known. Kenneth Porter documents their relations beginning in colonial New England and including the extensive contact in the South and the Indian Territory. He cites the anthropologist Melville J. Herskovits, who in the 1920s questioned 1,551 persons at Howard University and in Harlem, 33 per-

---

also Brown, *Archaeology of Mississippi*, 348. Today there are about 3,600 Choctaws, including both full and mixed bloods, on the surviving twenty-two square miles of tribal land, according to the *National Geographic School Bulletin*, LI (October 22, 1972), 99.

15. Faulkner, *The Sound and the Fury*, 7.

cent of whom claimed Indian blood. This figure may be above the facts—Porter thinks it is not—for a reason which makes Faulkner's character the more plausible. In the black community an Indian ancestor, unlike a white, was "a distinction to be trumpeted abroad from the housetops." [16]

If Porter is right about this, the phenomenon is not hard to understand in a culture which has extended to the indigenous, noble red man a theoretical respect denied the black, since before Jefferson's *Notes on Virginia*. The Indians were part of the land and they did not become the white man's slaves. [17] One of Langston Hughes's Simple stories, humorous comments on the black condition, makes fun of a man whose "uncle's cousin's great grandma were a Cherokee," and who attributes to this his temper, even his virility. He will not accept himself as black. [18] Murry Falkner recalls a black girl who "told me that she was born in a small town in Mississippi and brought here as a child. Later, when alone with my wife, she said that her ancestors were Indians from some island in the Caribbean Sea. . . . I never questioned her and I'm sure my brother would have acted the

16. Kenneth W. Porter, "Relations Between Negroes and Indians Within the Present Limits of the United States," *Journal of Negro History*, XVII (July, 1932), 287–88. Porter believes that Crispus Attucks had more Indian than Negro blood, and cites W. E. B. DuBois on the Indian blood of Frederick Douglass, 287–367 *passim*.

17. "Because the Negro labored, he was considered a draft animal. Because the Indian occupied large areas of land, he was considered a wild animal," Vine Deloria writes in *Custer Died for Your Sins* (New York, 1969), 11. Noting the widespread claims of Indian descent among whites, Deloria adds that the interest in Indian princess ancestors does not extend to the "wild" and threatening male.

18. Langston Hughes, "Simple on Indian Blood," in Langston Hughes and Arna Bontemps (eds.), *The Book of Negro Folklore* (New York, 1958), 612–15.

same." [19] There were mixed-blood communities in remote parts of the South, people with visible Indian traits who held themselves above the blacks. In the Sea Islands of Georgia such a man was called a "brass ankle," the title of a play by DuBose Heyward published, like "A Justice," in 1931. When Sam Fathers tells the white boy, "I was a warrior too then," his features and manner support the claim.

Faulkner had very probably heard someone like Sam talk. His Indian blood need not have been obvious to interest Faulkner, who would have responded not with Hughes's amusement, but with a willing imagination. Was it in boyhood, as in "A Justice" and "The Old People"? Both are told as memories, and the scenes in the shop at the farm are full of the boy's feeling for the old storyteller. The writer could have projected back in time a black friend like Earl Wortham, who shod his horses in later years. But Wortham's picture and conversation in the collection *William Faulkner of Oxford* reveal no trace of the Indian. And a passage in John Faulkner's memoir of his brother shows that there was a storytelling blacksmith at their grandfather's farm near Oxford, that as a boy William sat at his feet.

The description in *My Brother Bill* of the Falkners' Sunday excursions to the farm parallels the narrative frame of "A Justice". John Faulkner is not simply following the tale, which he elsewhere confuses with "Red Leaves." His memories have their own integrity. He tells how the younger children would run to the apple orchard or the peanut patch, while in "A Justice," being too young for man's talk, they are sent to the creek to fish—*The Sound and the Fury* had established the asso-

19. Murry Falkner to the author, December 29, 1972.

ciation of Caddy with the water. As in "A Justice," the older brother "would bear away from us as soon as he got in the gate, if he could hear the hammer ringing in the shed. He would be the last one back when Grandfather rounded us up to go home." Quentin is twelve at this point in the story, and Ike McCaslin first knows Sam Fathers at seven in "The Old People." John Faulkner, four years younger than William, supposes his brother was hearing hunting tales, and seems not to have known the man whom he calls "the Negro blacksmith." [20] Sam Fathers' first concern in both stories is to explain why he is not a Negro, and his features and manner are carefully compared and contrasted with the blacks'.

Faulkner could have imposed Indian blood upon his boyhood friend, of course. In Dilsey and her world in *The Sound and the Fury* he had anatomized the familiar face of the black, and when he wrote "A Justice" he was ready for a new departure. In Sam Fathers he transforms the old darky storytellers of southern nostalgia—the "inveterate old uncles of Joel Chandler Harris and Thomas Nelson Page," as they are called in Sterling Brown's survey of American Negro portraiture.[21] While subverting this stereotype he finds a way into the Indian world. He could have made up the character as he brings a few Chickasaws to life near the mound in "A Bear Hunt."

There are statistics of the U.S. government, however, which make Sam Fathers historically possible in Faulkner's country. A commission created by Congress in 1893 to assist the Five Civilized Tribes in the Indian Territory in the division of their tribal lands, found itself de-

20. John Faulkner, *My Brother Bill,* 72–73.
21. Sterling A. Brown, "A Century of Negro Portraiture in American Literature," *Massachusetts Review,* VII (Winter, 1966), 77.

nying the claims of thousands of so-called "Mississippi Choctaws," many of whom must have been part black. "In April of 1901, representatives of the Commission went to Mississippi, where . . . again they were deluged with applications from doubtful claimants." Of a total of 24,635 applications only 2,335 were accepted, those of full bloods and mixed bloods who could prove their ancestry. Some applicants were inspired by speculators and turned out to have no Indian blood at all. Others may have been descendants of the half-breeds, who, like Faulkner's Boon Hogganbeck, generally assimilated to the whites. But it was blacks who, in Indian Territory, constantly pressed for tribal status, wanting shares in the division of the land, while the tribes petitioned Congress against admitting them to the rolls. Choctaw freedmen claimed to be children of Choctaw fathers and black mothers. This is Sam Fathers' claim, and the numbers of rejected "Mississippi Choctaws" suggest that black Mississippians were making it.[22]

Not all need have been descendants of the Indians' slaves, given the Choctaw remnant in the state. Relations between blacks and Indians in the South continued. But if Sam Fathers was drawn from a Lafayette County man who had spent his adult life on the family farm as Sam had, he could plausibly derive himself from the earlier period. He may not have known much about what was happening in the Choctaw settlements a hundred miles away, but there was something in the air. Both of the state's senators—one the white supremacist Vardaman—

22. See Debo, *Choctaw Republic*, 274–76, and Edward Davis, "The Mississippi Choctaws," *Chronicles of Oklahoma*, X (June, 1932), 261, 263, 265–66. The figures are derived from the *Eleventh Annual Report of the Commission to the Five Civilized Tribes to the Secretary of the Interior* (Washington, D.C., 1904), 18–19.

had interested themselves in the cause of the depressed Mississippi Choctaws. In 1903, 264 full-blood Choctaws were moved by train to Indian Territory, and blacks with Indian blood may have seen this as the promised land.[23] That many were apparently claiming Indian identity shows once again how Faulkner knew and used his knowledge of his world. When Sam Fathers, shaping Ike's life, affirms the ritual of the wilderness and the hunt—when he who for two generations "had had to be a Negro" leaves the plantation to live in the big woods, echoing the spiritual as he says to McCaslin, "let me go"—the artist is working from social fact.

Sam Fathers says he is Choctaw in "A Justice." He is Chickasaw, and the son of Ikkemotubbe himself, in *Go Down, Moses*; yet the exposure of his body on the platform by Boon and Ike has been shown to be part of the distinctly Choctaw funeral ceremonies.[24] Taken as Faulkner's carelessness with detail, this suggests the adaptation of the old man's talk to the Chickasaw background of Lafayette County. The character becomes Chickasaw as the Indian material is transformed into myth, but his burial begins in the ancient Choctaw way, which serves Faulkner's dramatic needs and is what the Sam Fathers of "A Justice" would have wanted.

Faulkner's model, however, could scarcely have been the son of an Indian and a slave woman. He would have had to be born no later than the migrations of the 1830s, and there are earlier touches in the tale. The writer allows for this—"They said he was almost a hundred years old," the boy reflects. At such an age he would not have

23. *Eleventh Annual Report of the Commission*, 18–19.
24. Elmo Howell, "William Faulkner and the Chickasaw Funeral," *American Literature*, XXXVI (January, 1965), 523–35.

been very good at "making breast-yokes and wagon wheels." And, if half Indian, would he have to persuade the boy that he is not a black as the white people think? It has all the marks of a "stretcher," as Huck Finn would say. *Go Down, Moses* moves the action back into the 1880s. Sam Fathers can be acknowledged as an Indian by both blacks and whites—his mother becomes a quadroon, giving him white blood too—and is not too old to be a vigorous woodsman. But when Faulkner kills him off "A Justice" is left in the air.

Faulkner suggested the answer in response to Malcolm Cowley's worries about these "inconsistencies," which the editor wished to remove. He had telescoped two generations. "Had-Two-Fathers was the son of Doom and the slave woman in 'A Justice,' " he wrote Cowley. "Sam Fathers was actually Had-Two-Fathers' son, and hence the *grandson* of a king." [25] This is the case in the first, Harper's version of "The Old People," where royal lineage replaces the Indian father of "A Justice." Sam says his grandfather was Ikkemotubbe himself, which may have been the smith's alternate version. *Go Down, Moses* combines the two apocryphal tales. The evidence suggests that Sam Fathers was drawn from the grandson of an Indian and a slave, three-quarters black, his stories those his father had told him.

This is supported by the manuscript of "A Justice." The first page was apparently written before the others, and the opening phrase was initially "This is how my father [crossed out in favor of *pappy*] told it." In the published version Pappy is replaced by Herman Basket, the Indian from whom Sam has the story. There Faulkner

25. Faulkner to Malcolm Cowley, November, 1945, in Malcolm Cowley, *The Faulkner-Cowley File: Letters and Memories, 1944–1962* (New York, 1966), 54.

begins with an archetypal formula, "This is how Herman Basket told it when I was big enough to hear talk," then plunges into Doom's return from New Orleans to become chief. The manuscript contains a false start on the narrative. Doom is introduced through his boyhood will to hunt all night and fight for fun, in the days when "he and my pappy and Herman Basket were the same age, and slept on the same pallet." That is something one might remember first if told the story as a boy, something an old man could have said to engage his listener.[26]

III

There were also the lore the older Faulkner absorbed and his eclectic reading, which gave him impressions of the Indians in the southern frontier scene. Although he disclaimed "research," he believed that the author's reading should include history, biography, law, the whole record of man. "I wanted to learn about the South—that's why I read history," he said.[27] What he got from books merged with what he picked up from people, white and black. "Folklore blended together the Indian and the frontier as actual history had already done," a student of the background writes. "The backwoodsman conquered the Indian, but the Indian also conquered him," says Constance Rourke.[28]

26. Both quotations are from the manuscript of "A Justice" (MS in William Faulkner Collection, Alderman Library, University of Virginia), 1.

27. "Interview with Simon Claxton," in Meriwether and Millgate (eds.), *Lion in the Garden,* 280. For a denial that he read history, as quoted by Robert Cantwell, see "The Faulkners: Recollections of a Gifted Family," in Frederick J. Hoffman and Olga Vickery (eds.), *William Faulkner: Three Decades of Criticism* (East Lansing, Mich., 1960), 57. Faulkner did not want reporters like Cantwell learning about his life and habits.

28. Ward L. Miner, *The World of William Faulkner* (New York, 1952), 22; Constance Rourke, *American Humor: A Study of the National Character* (New York, 1953), 40.

Faulkner knew his way around the local Indian country at the beginning of the nineteenth century. Writing to Cowley from Hollywood in 1945 he drew a rough map including the Chickasaw-Choctaw boundary, the Choctaw agency, the river systems making New Orleans accessible and, on the east among the Chickasaws, Colbert's Ferry over the Tennessee. The old Natchez Trace ran southwest from Colbert's Ferry through the Mississippi Territory, an Indian trail which, after a treaty with the Chickasaws in 1801, became the wagon road by which the settlers came. In *Requiem for a Nun* the life of the Natchez Trace, with its bandits and its loyal postman, sets off Jefferson's emergence from a Chickasaw agency and trading post. The novel follows the founding of Oxford in 1836, and Faulkner's account of the dispossession of the Indians parallels the centennial issue of the Oxford *Eagle*. "The Chickasaw Indian woman, Ho-kah, No. 372, [who] affixed her signature, a cross-mark, to a deed" giving the land to the three founders of Oxford, becomes the bizarre and pathetic Mohataha.[29]

He was always eager to improve on the history he read. An aside on cannibalism, for example, adds to the moral horror of "Red Leaves." One of the old men who think slavery is ruining the tribe speaks of having tasted black flesh, and the council briefly wonders whether this is the solution to "the Negro question." At Virginia, Faulkner said that these Indians were not cannibals, but "who's to say whether at some time one of them might

29. Quoted from the Oxford *Eagle* in Elizabeth M. Kerr, *Yoknapatawpha: Faulkner's "Little Postage Stamp by Native Soil"* (New York, 1969), 83. Cf. William Faulkner, *Requiem for a Nun* (New York, 1951), 216–17. On the Natchez Trace and the Mississippi Territory, see also John A. Caruso, *The Southern Frontier* (Indianapolis and New York, 1963), 279–327.

have tried what it tasted like?" He took the funerary sacrifice in the story from a folktale without worrying about its historicity. It looks back to the Natchez, a remnant of whom had taken refuge among the Chickasaws of north Mississippi in the eighteenth century; and in their late Mississippi phase some Chickasaw conservatives, reacting against the missionaries, had tried to restore the old gods. So in this case fiction was within the bounds of possibility.[30]

His material included the story of Greenwood LeFlore, a French-descended Choctaw chief who, after helping arrange the Choctaw removal, had remained to become one of the richest cotton planters in the state. In his youth LeFlore had gone to Washington and faced down Andrew Jackson in a dispute over an Indian agent, an incident which provides the background for the White House demonstration in "Lo!" His legend was kept alive by the grandeur of his estate, Malmaison, about fifty miles south of Oxford.[31] Malmaison and the chief are brought in for color in the Civil War tale "Mountain

30. On the Natchez Indians, see Peter Farb, *Man's Rise to Civilization* (New York, 1968), 192–204. The persistence of their culture is attested by the discovery, in 1940, of two old people of Natchez ancestry living among the Cherokees, who spoke the old language. See *ibid*, 203.

31. See Allene De Shazo Smith, *Greenwood LeFlore and the Choctaw Indians of the Mississippi Valley* (Memphis, Tenn., 1951), and Mrs. N. D. Dupree, "Greenwood LeFlore," *Publications of the Mississippi Historical Society*, VII (Oxford, Miss., 1903), 141–51. At Virginia, Faulkner gave a short account of LeFlore's career, emphasizing the chief's shrewd acquisition of the tribal land (see Gwynn and Blotner [eds.], *Faulkner in the University*, 43–44), which parallels the account in *Mississippi: A Guide to the Magnolia State, Compiled and Written by the Federal Writers' Project* (New York, 1938), 403–405. In "Faulkner Borrows from the Mississippi Guide," *Mississippi Quarterly*, XIX (Summer, 1966), Thomas L. McHaney shows him incorporating whole paragraphs from this work in his fiction. But both "Lo!" and "Mountain Victory" appeared before the *Guide*, which told Faulkner what he already knew about the Indians.

Victory." This apparently early work suggests that an initially stale vision of the Old South contributed to Faulkner's interest in the Mississippi Indians.

In "Mountain Victory" a lushly glamorized Confederate officer returning from the war with his stereotyped comic black servant is ambushed by Unionist poor whites in Tennessee. The mountaineers are sharply realized in their attraction toward and hatred of the aristocrat, their fierce pride. The old regime comes to life only when the officer, Saucier Weddel, reveals himself as the son of the Choctaw chief of "Lo!" and master of Contalmaison, the plantation made from the tribal domain. He touches on his father's confrontation with President Jackson, then explains how the title of "the Man" has passed from their Europeanized and "polluted" branch of the family to a full-blooded Choctaw who lives in a cabin like those of the blacks. Faulkner had heard or read something about the divisions between mixed and full bloods, which scholars have come to stress.

In fact LeFlore was a Unionist who flew the stars and stripes over Malmaison throughout the war and was buried in the flag. The young Faulkner imposes the conventional southern mythology. The caricatured servant is literally the white man's burden, a dead weight that brings his master down; without his master's protection he is gunned down by their Negro-hating antagonists as the curtain falls. Weddel himself is all too ready to die—like Bayard Sartoris, he is a case of post–World War I angst identified with the "lost cause." Yet, interestingly, he is dark enough to be taken for a black, which provokes his account of his Choctaw blood. Faulkner saw the subversive possibilities of the Indian subject.

Local historical writing influenced his tales. Histories

of Mississippi begin with the Chickasaws and Choctaws, and the standard works lead one back to the accounts of travelers and missionaries and to the *Mississippi Territorial Archives*, a volume of which Faulkner owned. There are papers on the tribes in nearly every volume of the *Publications of the Mississippi Historical Society*, published in Oxford from 1900 to 1914. In one is a biography of Greenwood LeFlore, with a paragraph on LeFlore's trip to Washington to see Jackson. Another includes a description of the Choctaw funeral, in which the body was placed on a platform, as is Sam Fathers'; and nearby is a survey of his grandfather's efforts as a novelist which Faulkner must have seen. In a third volume one finds an account of the Colberts, mixed-blood Chickasaws alluded to in "A Courtship." The writer mentions a U.S. general's coat Andrew Jackson gave one of the Colbert men after the Creek War, and in "A Courtship" Ikkemotubbe has inherited such a coat from his uncle. Near this paper is a summary of Chickasaw marriage ritual, which was not much like Faulkner's florid courting competition. The scholarship was less a source than a stimulus of his work.[32]

32. In addition to Mrs. Dupree's paper on LeFlore, see H. S. Halbert, "Funeral Customs of the Choctaws," *Publications of the Mississippi Historical Society*, III (1900), 353–66, and Harry Warren, "Chickasaw Traditions, Customs, Etc.," and "Some Chickasaw Chiefs and Prominent Men," *ibid.*, VIII (1904), 543–53, 555–70. Faulkner owned Volume III of the *Mississippi Territorial Archives*, which was published after he began the Indian stories. Volume I, for the critical first years of the Mississippi Territory, had appeared in 1905, and there are traces of his familiarity with this work in the stories. He undoubtedly knew J. F. H. Claiborne's classic *Mississippi, as a Province, Territory, and State* (Jackson, Miss., 1880). He uses the French connection through New Orleans in his characterizations of Ikkemotubbe and Issetibbeha, and his sketches of the Indians jibe with Claiborne's descriptions. He may also have seen Cushman's standard *History of the Choctaw-Chickasaw, and Natchez Indians*, which draws on the accounts of earlier writers. There were studies of the

One is reminded of James's remark about the amount of history it takes to make a little literature. Faulkner could have heard about the Choctaw funeral and read about the general's coat in an account of Jackson's campaigns. Behind him was the older generation's interest in the Indians—the book in his library on the mounds, for example, was written by the elder Calvin S. Brown, Faulkner's French teacher at the university. There was the whole record of the Indian lost cause, in the South before the Civil War and in the West after, when Federal troops turned to assaulting Indian intransigents. He made his subject the murky period when tribal cultures were breaking down and the Indians mixing with white men and black. As the anthropologist Irving Hallowell points out, in America the theme of assimilation has been largely left to the imaginative writer.[33]

He both elaborates and undercuts the American romance of the Indian, going back to Crèvecoeur's statement, made much of by Lawrence, that "there must be in their social bond something singularly captivating, and far superior to anything to be boasted of among us; for thousands of Europeans are Indians, and we have no examples of even one of these aborigines having from choice become Europeans!"[34] "A Courtship" is in this

---

Chickasaws, of southeastern Indian ethnography, and the American Indian as slaveholder and secessionist in the years when Faulkner became interested in these subjects.

33. A. Irving Hallowell, "American Indians, White and Black: The Phenomenon of Transculturalization," *Current Anthropology*, IV (December, 1963), 520. Hallowell surveys the fiction about assimilation in this important article. In *The Course of Empire* (Boston, 1952), Chap. 4, Bernard De Voto notes that anthropologists have neglected the period of white contact.

34. J. Hector St. Jean de Crèvecoeur, *Letters from an American Farmer* (New York, 1957), 209. This is quoted by D. H. Lawrence, *Studies in Classic American Literature* (New York, 1953), 42–43. Crèvecoeur, how-

tradition, "Red Leaves" a radical critique of it. In the four stories the red men evolve toward the dominant white culture, while "The Bear" gives us both the Indian who will not assimilate—Sam Fathers is a descendant of Freneau's "Indian Student"—and the black who prefers an Indian ancestry. Through the southern experience Faulkner treats varieties of what Hallowell calls "transculturalization."

As slavery shapes the Indian world in "Red Leaves" and "A Justice," so the black past contributes to the hunting ritual of *Go Down, Moses.* Indeed, there are echoes of an African priestly-patriarchal tradition in the cult of the forest and training of the initiate. If Sam Fathers was drawn from the grandson of a slave among the Indians, whose slaves enjoy cultural freedom even in "Red Leaves," he could have kept alive something of his African past, representing it to the boy as Indian. One need not assume this to explain the ambience of black Mississippi in "The Bear." Faulkner knew no Indians, while blacks outnumber whites in Lafayette County, and in still larger proportions in Yoknapatawpha.[35]

The greeting of "Oleh, Grandfather" at the center of his Indian legend marks his synthesizing imagination. The word *oleh* has no apparent Indian root. It is first spelled *olé*, yet the meaning is not quite that of the Spanish exclamation of appreciation. It may be demotic Spanish for *Hola* or *Ola* (the *h* is silent), a general greet-

---

ever, reversed himself upon closer acquaintance with the Indians, repudiating the noble savage for the barbarian of the captivity narratives. See his *Voyage dans la Haute Pennsylvanie,* (Paris, 1801), I, 95–96 and as translated by H. N. Fairchild, *The Noble Savage: A Study in Romantic Naturalism* (New York, 1928), 103.

35. See inclusive bibliography in William R. Ferris, Jr., *Mississippi Black Folklore* (Hattiesburg, Miss., 1971).

ing common in the Spanish Caribbean.[36] Louisiana, whence Doom returns with the slaves in "A Justice," had been Spanish for the last three decades of the eighteenth century. *Oleh* also resembles words for authority, protection, and honor in several West African languages, and its first speaker is not Sam Fathers but the slave in "Red Leaves" who was brought from Africa at the age of fourteen.[37] Faulkner may have made it up, or he may have remembered something he had heard, assimilating it to *olé* when he learned Spanish, then changing the spelling so it would not be misunderstood.[38]

The "Grandfather" in the phrase comes from his reading about the Indians. Numerous tribes have addressed

36. Arturo Cuyás *et al.*, *Appleton's Revised English-Spanish and Spanish-English Dictionary* (New York, 1956), Pt. 2, p. 302.

37. There are striking parallels with Yoruba, the language of West Nigeria and background of much of the Spanish Caribbean. In Yoruba *oloye* means most honored one, and the *y* could easily have dropped out, leaving a sound like *oloeh*. *Ola* is the honor shown or due to a person, and its variations may include *olala* and *olela*, the honorable or respected. *Olú* means chief or lawgiver, and can become part of an individual's name, to be passed on to his son and grandson. See T. J. Bowen, "Grammar and Dictionary of the Yoruba Language, with an Introductory Description of the Country and the People of Yoruba," *Smithsonian Contributions to Knowledge* (Washington, D.C., 1858), X, and R. C. Abrahams, *Dictionary of Modern Yoruba* (London, 1970). Mr. Christian Olúsoji Adeyosoye, a student at Howard University, explained to me how *olú* can be passed on in a chief's family, and Mr. Henry Drewel, a student at Teachers College, Columbia University, explained the variations of *ola* and the way the Yoruba noun is used in the sense of an exclamation. Not many Yoruba-speaking slaves were imported into the United States in the eighteenth century, but a large proportion of the total number came from Angola and Senegambia, countries in whose languages one can find comparable words. For the origins of American slaves, see Philip D. Curtin, *The Atlantic Slave Trade* (Madison, Wisc., 1969), especially 144, fig. 12. I am indebted to Robert F. Thompson, professor of art and director of the undergraduate program in black studies, Yale University, for perspective on the possibilities of linguistic derivation and on the African dimension of "The Old People" and "The Bear."

38. Faulkner's biographer writes that Faulkner knew Spanish. Joseph L. Blotner to the author, September 27, 1971.

the rattlesnake as "Chief" (of serpents) and "Grand-father," and used the terms for other totem animals, as Sam Fathers does with the great antlered deer in "The Old People." [39] Faulkner amalgamates this with what he learned of primitive cultures in Frazer's *Golden Bough*, an influence on "Red Leaves" and *Go Down, Moses*. He adapts his reading to his own tradition. Whereas the totemism of "Red Leaves" is resonant but matter of fact, the snake at the end of "The Bear" is the "old one" from the Garden of Eden.

Such synthesis was only possible for an earnest believer in the unity of man. "There is no such thing as an 'Anglo-Saxon' heritage and an African heritage," Faulkner said. "There is the heritage of man. Nothing is extinct in any race, only dormant. You are brave and tough when you have to be. You are intelligent when the age demands it. There are all things in like degree in all races." [40] His aim is to break down the barriers of race and class and time as Sam Fathers is said to in "The Old People":

And as he talked about those old times and those dead and vanished men of another race from either that the boy knew, gradually to the boy those old times would cease to be old times and would become a part of the boy's present, not only as if they happened yesterday but as if they were still happening, the men who walked through them actually walking in breath and air and casting an actual shadow on the earth they had not quitted. And more: as

39. See Laurence M. Klauber, *Rattlesnakes: Their Habits, Life Histories, and Influence on Mankind* (Berkeley, 1956), II, 1085–96. Calvin S. Brown called my attention to this book, which is more detailed than the anthropological studies of totemism. Mr. Brown also corroborates my fruitless search for words like *oleh* in the Chickasaw and Choctaw glossaries. Calvin S. Brown to the author, October 28, 1971.

40. "Interview with Russell Warren Howe," in Meriwether and Millgate (eds.), *Lion in the Garden*, 264.

if some of them had not happened yet but would occur
tomorrow, until at last it would seem to the boy that he
himself had not come into existence yet, that none of his
race nor the other subject race which his people had
brought with them into the land had come here yet . . .
and that it was he, the boy, who was the guest here and
Sam Fathers' voice the mouthpiece of the host.

Faulkner's tales do not return us to the world before the
white men came, but they expand our past and give perspective on a later American scene. To take them together is to see how much this corner of his work includes.
It is a long way from "Lo!" and "A Courtship" to "The
Bear," but the lighter stories have their special charm,
and the order of the chronicle is one of ascending intensity and achievement. His passage is full of the mystery
of art, and the work bears him out.

III. "Lo!"

The least serious of the stories is the most contemporary in subject. "Lo!" evokes the response of the Indians to white encroachment, and it is the first American fiction to describe a sit-in. It will surely remain the most fanciful. Written in the early thirties, in the context of the bonus marches and other mass movements of the time, the story brings a whole Chickasaw tribe to Washington seeking ceremonial exoneration for the murder of a too-ambitious trader. They are camped on the White House lawn in army tents slashed open at the top to serve as tepees, and the countryside through which they have passed is in an uproar. Under seige the president and secretary give the old chief what he wants, then see the whole thing happening again. Faulkner explodes the notion of Indian naïveté, suspending the perspective of history in which the red men lose their lands. "Lo!" is a tall tale of how you can "fight City Hall," written with a southerner's appreciation of the discomfiture of Washington power. It is a situation comedy with broad elements of farce, which anticipates the confrontation politics of our time.

The story is worthy of a close reading, for it shows how Faulkner uses history, and it introduces his idea of the Indian as neither Hiawatha nor a savage with a tomahawk, conceptions which had rationalized the white man's advance. The successful tribesmen of "Lo!" are a people philosophical, shrewd, funny, and likely to have the last laugh. They evidently go back to the lines about the Indian in Pope, whom Faulkner enjoyed and in this instance used as a point of departure:

> Lo, the poor Indian! whose untutored mind
> Sees God in clouds, or hears him in the wind;
> His soul proud Science never taught to stray
> Far as the solar walk or milky way;
> Yet simple nature to his hope has giv'n
> Behind the cloud-topt hill, an humbler Heav'n,
> Some safer world in depth of woods embraced,
> Some happier island in the wat'ry waste,
> Where slaves once more their native land behold,
> No fiends torment, no Christians thirst for gold.
> To be, contents his natural desire;
> He asks no Angel's wing, no Seraph's fire;
> But thinks, admitted to that equal sky,
> His faithful dog shall bear him company.[1]

Pope is affirming natural religion and deistic common sense, but on behalf of the original Mississippians and as a man with the frontier in his bones Faulkner objects to the image. The chief mockingly calls himself and his people "poor ignorant Indians"—he repeats the word ignorant—here today and gone tomorrow, scarcely presuming to take up the time of such busy white men. Lo, Faulkner says, here are some Indians in our American humor.

The president's face, in the opening lines, wears "an

1. "Essay on Man," Espistle I:111, lines 99–112, *Selected Writings of Alexander Pope* (New York, 1933), 69.

expression of humorless concern, since humor had departed from his situation and his view of it almost three
weeks before." He is standing at his dressing-room door
using a lady's hand-mirror to see through the crack down
the corridor, and what he first sees is a bone with the
mark of human teeth on it. Two Chickasaws squat there
in beaver hats and new frock coats and knee breeches,
their neatly rolled pants and their boots on the floor beside their naked feet. Outfitted at his expense, as it turns
out, they speak of the strangeness of "white man's honor,"
which requires "guests to squat all night long in the cold
outside this man's door." It is winter and snowing; they
have been there for three weeks and are prepared to wait
until spring. Other Indians from up and down the frontier are coming to join them, causing havoc en route.

This absurd scene evokes the young agrarian republic
where police lines did not exist and those who came to
see the Great White Father were not turned away. "Even
Jackson, who enjoyed warm personal relations with many
individual Indians, kept what amounted to an open
house for Indian visitors." [2] LeFlore was hospitably received by Jackson, according to the Historical Society account which Faulkner may have seen, and the president
gave in to the Choctaw chief, saying, "Greenwood, we
have been friends too long to fall out now." [3] At this
point Faulkner departs from the tale, allowing no such
bond to cloud the questions at issue. His principals represent opposed cultures, a grave, patriarchal community
against a restless people already committed to capitalist

2. Dale Van Every, *Disinherited: The Lost Birthright of the American
Indian* (New York, 1966), 36.
3. Mrs. N. D. Dupree, "Greenwood LeFlore," *Publications of the Mississippi Historical Society*, VII (Oxford, Miss., 1903), 145.

ownership. The president, like Jackson a general, gives in to restore order, and so his wife can again receive the French ambassador's wife.

As for the Indians' capacity to make such nuisances of themselves, Faulkner may have been reading in the *Mississippi Territorial Archives* for 1798 to 1803, when the first settlers were entering his part of the country. Both governors for these years complain of Choctaws who descend on Natchez with requests and remain until they get their way, embarrassing officials and distressing the inhabitants. Claiborne writes to James Madison in 1802:

> I continue to be much harassed with Visits from my Choctaw Brethren;—these poor, Idle and humble People are really great pests to this territory;—I suppose at this moment there cannot be less, than two or three hundred, (consisting of Men, Women, & children) Encamped within six miles around Natchez, & for a support, they almost *entirely* depend upon begging and stealing; the Citizens who experience frequent losses in Cattle & Hogs, are becoming highly dissatisfied, & I find it difficult to *shield* the *Indians from much violence.*[4]

Faulkner's Chickasaws do not steal or beg. Respectable folk who can clearly take care of themselves, they hunt deer on foot with their knives and bring the carcasses onto the White House grounds. The historical Choctaws wanted ammunition and presents from Claiborne and managed to get whiskey from the citizens, while the Indians of Yoknapatawpha are never debauched by alcohol. But the tribe is there—men, women, children, and slaves

4. Claiborne to James Madison, April 3, 1802, in *Mississippi Territorial Archives*, I (1798–1803), ed. Dunbar Rowland (Nashville, Tenn., 1905), 402.

—and the citizens of the whole eastern seaboard are pressing the government to get them out.

Faulkner makes the dispute turn on the fundamental issue absent in these sources, that of the white man's property lust, and makes his Indians too smart and tough to be victims of this. The background as reviewed for the president is a droll parable. A trader came and gave the Chickasaws money for some land, containing, as they later realized, the only entrance to a river ford; fenced this off, and established a tollgate; bought a horse with his first proceeds, and successfully raced it against the chief's nephew's horse, "the wager the ford and tollgate against a thousand or so acres of land." "All the Southern Indians were addicted to gambling and betting," and would risk their territories on important occasions, according to a classic history of Mississippi.[5] But Faulkner's tribe is not willing to lose this time, having seen the man's fence and tollgate. The night after winning the race he has died of a split skull. While the federal agent perfunctorily investigates the murder, the old chief brings his nephew to Washington to receive judgment from the president himself. It is a formal ceremonial submission which puts authority on notice.

The story anticipates Ikkemotubbe's original sin of selling the land in "The Bear," but in the prelapsarian world of "Lo!" the Indians can kill the buyer and get it back. They plainly know what they are doing when it

5. J. F. H. Claiborne, *Mississippi, as a Province, Territory, and State* (Jackson, Miss., 1880), 485. "At their ball plays, they bet their ponies, their crops, their clothing, and their trinkets, and in a game between two tribes, they would sometimes stake a part of the territories that they claimed. The Creeks and Choctaws had several international games in which territory was lost and won, sometimes resulting in war." One sees from Faulkner's tale how this ethos historically played into the white man's hands.

all happens a second time, with the chief wryly writing
to the president about the curious behavior of the whites.
He articulates the tribal opposition to the property con-
cept by which, historically, Indians were victimized. In
"Lo!" they resist in their own way, by murder and appeal
to the paternalism of the white chief. They manipulate
the enemy through his image of Indian innocence and
childishness.

This is an alternative to the history in the novels and
"The Bear." The Compson and Sutpen dynasties are
founded on the Indian passion for horse racing, and the
operations of these future aristocrats are much like the
fleecing of Frenchman's Bend by the Snopeses. Faulkner
knows the sources of power in his world. He derives it
from the bargaining and gambling that enlivened rural
life, from the contest of the Yankee trader with the folk,
also stressed in *American Humor*.[6] There is a characteristic vignette in "Lo!" of the Indians watching the white
entrepreneur, who worked in the sun to build his fence,
sitting in the shade to collect. "He had a deerskin pouch
fastened to a post for the travellers to drop their coins in,
and the gate itself arranged so he could operate it by a
rope from the veranda of his one-room domicile without
having to even leave his seat." It is the only time in
Faulkner that the character doesn't get away with it.

He doesn't because the story is an entertainment in
which the writer's realism is relaxed, a joke on history as
well as on the government. Only on this level, in 1934,
could he see the Indians getting their own back. Their

6. Constance Rourke, *American Humor: A Study of the National Character* (New York, 1953), 15–17. The book begins with this figure and story.
First published in 1931, it is another manifestation of the context in
which Faulkner worked.

conversation is a put down of the whites and reversal of racist condescension: "You don't understand white people. They are like children: you have to handle them careful because you never know what they are going to do next. . . . So as long as we are here, we'll have to try to act like these people believe that Indians ought to act. Because you never know until afterward just what you have done to insult or scare them. Like this having to talk white talk all the time." Faulkner had heard blacks talked about this way, and his use of the red man to satirize his own people goes back through Franklin to Voltaire and Montaigne. "Savages we think them, because their manners differ from ours, which we think the perfection of civility; they think the same of theirs." So Franklin wrote in 1782.[7]

The historical position of the southern tribes between their traditional culture and the white man makes this dialogue plausible, but Faulkner's Chickasaws turn the tables without regard for probabilities. In return for what are called their Pickwickian costumes they have given the president a ridiculous gold uniform, formally presenting it in his bedroom at five o'clock in the morning. Against these exasperating characters, who are well mannered and do not know their place, are authorities who bear the red man's burden of innocence and helplessness. The president and his staff have Faulkner's sympathy, confronted by a people they do not understand. They are too frustrated for villains and, until the end of

7. Benjamin Franklin, "Remarks Concerning the Savages of North America," in H. H. Smyth (ed.), *The Writings of Benjamin Franklin* (New York, 1905–1907), X, 97–104. See also F. M. A. de Voltaire, *L'Ingenu de Voltaire* (Paris, 1936), and "Of Cannibals," in *The Essays Of Montaigne*, ed. E. J. Trechmann (New York, n.d.), 202–14.

the story, too passive to match the interest of the Indians on the attack.

With the president he ranges from mock epic, taking down "the soldier chief of a party and a nation," to devices of domestic comedy, like sending him down the backstairs of the White House in his stockinged feet. At the secretary of state's house the two men review the affair in their "baffled outrage," the secretary a straight man to his boss, who is his own straight man. Merely put out, they affect to beat their heads against the wall of fate like true Faulknerians. "Lo!" anticipates the scene in *The Hamlet* where the Devil and his lieutenant react to Flem Snopes's demands, but in Washington, Faulkner lacks the imaginative freedom he has in Hell. Nor can he give us history itself—the determined Jackson who is said to have remarked of the Supreme Court decision supporting the Cherokees' right to their land, "John Marshall has made his decision, now let him enforce it." [8]

The president never quite grasps the Indians' purpose in coming, and the old chief takes charge the moment he is introduced. Half Chickasaw, half Frenchman, he is the ideal opposite of Pope's Indian, a human eel too slippery to be caught by Washington hands:

> The soft, paunchy man facing them with his soft, bland, inscrutable face—the long, monk-like nose, the slumbrous lids, the flabby, *café-au-lait*-colored jowls above a froth of soiled lace of an elegance fifty years outmoded and vanished; the mouth was full, small, and very red. Yet somewhere behind the face's expression of flaccid and weary disillusion, as behind the bland voice and the almost fem-

8. Van Every, *Disinherited*, 160. See also Peter Farb, *Man's Rise to Civilization* (New York, 1968), 301.

inine mannerisms, there lurked something else: something willful, shrewd, unpredictable and despotic.

The vision is Faulkner's own, but the chief's background is broadly representative. LeFlore was the son of Louis LeFleur, French trader and trapper, and Rebecca Crevat, the niece of Pushmataha, greatest of Choctaw chiefs. The Creek chief Alexander McGillivray, a Scotsman's son whose brilliant diplomacy protected the southern Indians in the post-Revolutionary period, was part French on his mother's side and is the subject of a memoir published in Paris.[9] The North American tribes were full of half-breeds whose fathers had responded to the "social bond" of which Crèvecoeur speaks, and the sons were Indians in all respects but color.[10] In language that has something of the flavor of Faulkner's character, Tocqueville complains that his nation "too often grew passionately fond of Indian life. They became the most dangerous inhabitants of the wilderness." [11]

Faulkner's chief, Francis Vidal or Weddel—the authorities don't know which to use, and he gives them no help—knows his tactics like a veteran confrontationist and at once objects to meeting in the secretary's house instead of the White House. Holding the nephew's arm, he

9. Louis Milfort, *Memoire ou coup d'oeil rapide sur mes différens voyages et mon sejour dans la nation Creek* (Paris, 1802). See also John W. Caughey, *McGillivray of the Creeks* (Norman, Okla., 1938).

10. A. Irving Hallowell, "American Indians, White and Black: The Phenomenon of Transculturization," *Current Anthropology*, IV (December, 1963), especially 526–27, stresses the receptivity of Indian societies.

11. Alexis de Tocqueville, *Democracy in America* (New York, 1954), I, 359. Miner suggests that "the intimate relations between the French and the Indians [in Mississippi] . . . is more folklore than actual history." Ward L. Miner, *The World of William Faulkner* (New York, 1952), 90. There may be a confusion here between the Chickasaws of Faulkner's country and the Choctaws to the south and west, who had been deeply involved with the French, a premise of "A Justice" and "Red Leaves."

smilingly requests exoneration in a form that is half admission, half threat. "If this white man really did not fall from that swift horse of his perhaps and strike his head upon a sharp stone, then this nephew of mine should be punished. We do not think that it is right to slay white men like a confounded Cherokee or Creek." Faulkner jokes at the law-and-order rhetoric of the whites, and again he may have been reading the *Mississippi Archives*. Governor Claiborne writes as follows to an influential person among the Choctaws: "It is true there are ill-disposed men in all nations, and that mischief from such persons cannot at all times be prevented. But when a man commits an offence, and is punished for it, he will take care not to do so again. . . . That is the reason why the white men punish their bad men with such severity." [12] The secretary fails to match the Indian's suave ironies. "You should have held this horse-race across the ford itself. Water wouldn't have left that gash in the white man's skull," he says. To which the reply is, "But this white man would doubtless have required a coin of money from my nephew for passing through his gate." The chief is not satisfied with a written statement of the nephew's innocence, and he is properly irritated with the president's remark that "my Indian and white people are the same." Their affair should then be concluded in the capitol. He can wait until May, if the building will not be free till then. He will have to wait anyway, since more of his people are arriving.

Time, ironically, has transformed this from the fantasy it must have seemed to early readers. From Alcatraz to the Indian Bureau in Washington to Wounded Knee, Faulk-

12. Claiborne to John Pitchylynn, *Mississippi Territorial Archives*, I, 488.

ner anticipates our symbolic politics and revolution-as-
theater. His humor, which dates the story, gives him aesthetic distance. He is not out to justify either side. His
vision of democracy recalls Mencken's but is not sour.

The burlesque capitulation follows. A strange proces-
sion moves down Pennsylvania Avenue through the winter snow and on into a meeting of the House of Representatives: "So it was that behind the Speaker's desk of
that chamber which was to womb and contemplate the
high dream of a destiny superior to the injustice of events
and the folly of mankind, the President and the Secretary
stood, while below them, ringed about by the living ma-
nipulators of, and interspersed by the august and watching ghosts of the dreamers of the destiny, the uncle and
nephew stood, with behind them the dark throng of kin
and friends and acquaintances." In his law Latin, the
president intones ten sonnets from a volume of Petrarch
snatched up from the secretary's table, then signals for
an artillery salute outside. Luckily the guns, unused since
the revolutionary war, do not explode and bring on his
impeachment. Faulkner is the Mark Twain of *A Con-
necticut Yankee* minus the fascination with technology
and "working the crowd." He smiles at the Latin verse
and old cannon and at the protesters impressed by the
symbols of power.[13] He evokes the exuberant youth of
the country and the resilience of its institutions.

One can imagine the Indian stories adapted to the
stage as Lowell does "Benito Cereno" in *The Old Glory,*

13. Here Faulkner turns history to farce. The great Choctaw chief
Pushmataha had died in Washington while representing his people, and
according to Chief David Folsom, Pushmataha's last request of President
Jackson was, "Let the big guns be fired over me." Allene De Shazo Smith,
Greenwood LeFlore and the Choctaw Indians of the Mississippi Valley
(Memphis, Tenn. 1951), 48.

but this scene would be modified. The authorities could not be so boyishly naïve, the sound of Latin and of guns might survive as the death knell of western civilization. The Indians could merely pretend to be impressed—putting on the man—and let us know their victory is modest or illusory. When they get home it will all begin again anyway. And so it does, but these Indians are scarcely innocent victims. The next fall, in a mellow satisfaction with the state of the land, the president receives the letter which creates the coda. "Dear Sir and Friend: This is really amusing," it begins, Faulkner's way around the rule against laughing at your own stories: "Again this hot-headed nephew—he must have taken his character from his father's people, since it is none of mine—has come to trouble you and me. It is this cursed ford again. Another white man came among us, to hunt in peace we thought, since God's forest and the deer which He put in it belong to all. But he too became obsessed with the idea of owning this ford." Chuckling sadly, Weddel tells how the second buyer of the ford staked it against "a few miles of land" in a swimming race with the nephew. "Unfortunately our white man failed to emerge from the river until after he was dead." The tribe is on its way to Washington again. As the curtain closes the president dons the general's mantle, with desperate glee marshaling troops and preparing to head them off en route. It is a burlesque of the Indian campaigns.

The chief's communalism, which anticipates "The Bear," shows Faulkner had been reading Rousseau on the origins of inequality. "You are lost," Rousseau concludes, in a passage from which Isaac McCaslin's vision stems, "if you forget that the fruits of the earth belong equally to us all, and the earth itself to nobody." [14] We may note that this perspective comfortably coexists with slaveholding, which is common to the Chickasaw culture and the white. Slavery does not justify the dispossession of the tribes, as in the severer moral vision of "The Bear." Nor does Faulkner destroy the myth of benevolent white paternalism, with which he has such fun. The President's last act is a proclamation he knows has no legal force, that no white may "buy, lease, or accept the ford as a gift," and that anyone crossing it in either direction does so at his own risk. In language which owes something to the civil rights controversy in the South, M. E. Bradford calls this the failure of "an abstract and ideologically rigid central authority" to give equal justice to the variety of its people.[15] This seems too abstract and ideological for Faulkner's scene, while the story's premises include the dependence of the Indians on Washington as against the land-hungry settlers.

Yet the final breakdown of authority and faint echo of the Civil War place the tale in a southern frame. Faulkner's Chickasaws are more than objects of an amused provincial pride. Allen Tate has remarked on his use of "the Greco-Trojan myth (Northerners as the upstart Greeks, Southerners as the older, more civilized Trojans) . . . a large semi-historical background against which even his ignorant characters, like Lena Grove or Dewey Dell Bundren, as well as the more civilized Compsons or Sartorises,

14. J. J. Rousseau, *First and Second Discourses*, ed. Roger O. Masters (New York, 1964) 141–42.

15. M. E. Bradford, "Faulkner and the Great White Father," *Louisiana Studies* (Northwestern State College), III (1964), 323–29. Bradford believes that Faulkner indicts "misguided federalism" and "uniformitarian Jacobin abstractions."

could be projected in more than human dimensions." [16]
As Tate suggests, his imagination extends the myth in un-
expected ways. One notes the comparison of Old Ben to
Priam in "The Bear." He destroys smug assumptions—
Tate's use of "ignorant" may be contrasted with the
Chickasaw chief's humor on this subject. The Indians
are the Trojans of the tale, their opponents in Washington and Mississippi the Greeks, representatives of a brash
young culture.

These Trojans are not southern gentlemen but people
who would drown you in a swimming race, who leave
bones on your rug. Their South is that of the frontier.
Yet theirs is the older, wiser civilization, as Faulkner
shows. They will nonetheless succumb to the delusion of
property and, like the civilization to follow them, they
are doomed, although they may win a few battles. The
Indians as aggressors invading the citadel that the admin-
istration defends show how the writer divides his Trojan
sympathies to make a good story. He is not too southern
to identify with the nation first—with that "dream of a
destiny superior to the injustice of events and the folly
of mankind," the impossibility of which his comedy
illustrates.

16. From Allen Tate's summing-up on Faulkner in "Appendix: Notes
and Comments," in Robert Penn Warren (ed.), *Faulkner: A Collection of
Critical Essays* (Engelwood Cliffs, N. J., 1966), 276.

IV ❧ "A Courtship"

"A Courtship" is Faulkner's romance of reconciliation, his version of the heroic age when manhood transcended race. Humor is now allied to sentiment, the lethal contest of "Lo!" transformed into a ritual of brotherhood. The young Ikkemotubbe and David Hogganbeck, a riverboat pilot, compete for the love of Herman Basket's sister by feats of endurance which make them friends and ultimately involve them in saving one another's lives. Ironically, the girl chooses a third suitor, the unheroic Log-in-the-Creek, whose devotion is to her alone. The rude awakening of the other two sends them out of the "Plantation" into the white world, from which, we are told, Ikkemotubbe seven years later returns as the cold and ruthless ruler Doom. Faulkner creates a strenuous idyll to introduce and set off the tribal experience of "A Justice" and "Red Leaves."

The story looks back to Cooper, *Moby-Dick*, and *Huckleberry Finn*, where racial brotherhood is bound up with nostalgia for the receding frontier and withdrawal from woman and society. In "The Bear" Faulkner makes this theme his own, and "A Courtship," the only one of the Indian stories written after "The Bear," extends it into the past, the old days, far from the South

he knew. As the white man's capital is the proper setting
for the conflict of cultures in "Lo!," the Indian stage is
appropriate for the rendering of harmony and assimilation. Faulkner's Indians are most like noble savages in
"A Courtship." The tall tale is fused with the gentle-
manly conventions of the epic. But he also has the local
history in mind.

The period between the border wars and the beginnings of Indian removal has been characterized as one of
peaceful progress on the southern frontier, when Indian
and backwoodsman came to know each other's ways:
"Interracial friendships developed. White men gained
permission to live in Indian communities where their
presence was doubly welcomed were they able to teach
Indians craft skills such as metal-working and woodwork-
ing or how to read and write. Indians readily found em-
ployment on the white side of the border or were as
readily received as respected guests in white homes."
The writer speaks of "the interplay of instinctive sympathies between red and white hunter-farmers." [1] The
new attitude achieved political expression in the lifelong
championship of Indian rights by two of the great figures
of the time, Davy Crockett and Sam Houston. They were
frontiersmen like Jackson, and neither hesitated to defy
him over the issue.

Sam Houston's relationship with the Indians recalls
Crèvecoeur's appreciation of their "singularly gratifying
social bond." For the architect of Texas independence
the Cherokees provided a second home. When his young
bride left him, he resigned the governorship of Tennessee, became a Cherokee citizen, and took a Cherokee

1. Dale Van Every, *Disinherited: The Lost Birthright of the American Indian* (New York, 1966), 35–36.

woman as his new wife. In his youth, Houston had run away to live for two years with the Cherokees, "forming lasting friendships among their young warriors, courting their girls, winning the affectionate regard of their chiefs." [2] He took Pope's *Iliad* along and claimed that an Indian foster brother learned English from hearing him read it. In his autobiography, calling these his happiest years, he dwells on the grace and simplicity of Indian courtship.[3]

Faulkner's courtship is a different matter, however. Whereas Houston relished the complaisance of the "Indian maidens," and could dispose of any competition, he says, by properly petitioning the gods, Herman Basket's sister is aloof and self-directed, and the rivals practically kill themselves for her favor. Faulkner adapts the contest of the suitors to the Indian scene, via the southwestern contest stories, like Longstreet's "The Fight." He transplants the ritual of courtly love, which transforms the lover into a hero, in the American world where the girl may not want a hero and where she has her way. Against this humorous backdrop the struggle of Ikkemotubbe and Hogganbeck succeeds in releasing deeper feelings than either has about the girl. The real courtship is between them.

This is one theme of Fiedler's *Love and Death in the American Novel,* and Elmo Howell reads the story in Fiedler's terms, contrasting Herman Basket's sister's marriage with "the main love affair . . . that which develops

---

2. *Ibid.,* 36. See also Marquis James, *The Raven: A Biography of Sam Houston* (Dunwoody, Ga., 1968), especially "Deer Tracks and Tape" and "Exile."

3. Sam Houston, *The Autobiography of Sam Houston,* ed. Donald Day and Harry Herbert Ullom (Norman, Okla., 1954), 5–6.

between the two males." [4] He could have cited the Freudian symbolism at the climax of the tale, when the men are trying to help each other out of a collapsing cave. Yet "A Courtship" is conventionally masculine in feeling. Ikkemotubbe and Hogganbeck are immature and readier for friendship than for love but committed to their female prey. Their attachment across the racial barrier lacks the larger subversive implications Fiedler finds in our classical fiction. "A Courtship" is an evocation of radical innocence, projected upon the Indian world before its corruption by the white man's ways.

It is an easy work to underestimate, relaxed, graceful, almost slick, a late literary imitation of oral tradition. The narrative voice, supposedly that of an Indian looking back to the old days, to his father's youth, is a more obvious mask for Faulkner than Sam Fathers' voice, and is sometimes precious and sentimental. Its strengths are a humorous perspective and a flowing rhythm of incantation appropriate to the heroic past. The nostalgia for the days when men were men, an authentic mark of the folk culture, lends itself to the middle-aged writer's nostalgias, while the comic spirit keeps the latter in hand.

A jocular beginning places the story after "Lo!" in Faulkner's chronicle. "The People all lived in the Plantation now," inside a boundary agreed to by the chief and General Jackson. Killing even a worthless white man on the wrong side of this imaginary line through the forests "became what the white men called a crime punishable by death if they could just have found who did it." Faulkner sees the Indians through the lawless tradi-

4. Elmo Howell, "Inversion and the 'Female' Principle: William Faulkner's 'A Courtship,'" *Studies in Short Fiction*, IV (Summer, 1967), 310 and *passim*.

tion of Frenchman's Bend and Beat Four. His horizon expands as he describes their bounteous land—"this land for which, as Issetibbeha used to say after he had become so old that nothing more was required of him except to sit in the sun and criticize the degeneration of the People and the folly and rape of politicians, the Great Spirit has done more and man less than for any land he ever heard of." The land in question is America, and the chief's voice is that of Mencken and Mark Twain, and of the old poet of a world "where every prospect pleases, and only man is vile." [5]

Herman Basket's sister is introduced as one of the pleasing prospects, an Indian Eula Varner, a comic match for Byron's heroine. "Because she walked in beauty. Or she sat in it, that is, because she did not walk at all unless she had to." She does not like to bathe either, but she changes Ikkemotubbe's life. There is a before-and-after picture, repeated at the end of "A Courtship," of what the young Indian is and what he will become. One day, having known the girl since he was two years old, he saw her for the first time, and one night when it was all over he left the plantation, to return as the self-determined Doom. Faulkner may be glancing back at his first, disappointed love for Estelle Oldham, whom he had known since he was two and lost at twenty to another man. Ten years later he won her back, when he had become the author of *The Sound and the Fury*.

There is nothing here of Chickasaw courtship as he may have read of it in Claiborne or in the *Publications of the Mississippi Historical Society*—a modest affair in which the woman displayed her consent or lack of same

5. "From Greenland's Icy Mountains," a missionary hymn familiar to southerners of the past, written by Reginald Heber (1783–1826).

by how fast she ran with the man pursuing her.[6] Ikke-motubbe's wooing is all competitive display. First with his body "oiled with bear's grease as when racing," then "wearing his flower-painted weskit and pigeon-tailed coat and beaver hat in which he looked handsomer than a steamboat gambler and richer even than the whiskey-trader," he parades on his various horses past the porch where Herman Basket's sister sits, shelling corn or peas into the silver wine pitcher inherited from her proudest female relative. Faulkner's Indians have been absorbing the white man's mores and his goods. Ikkemotubbe tries to buy her family's favor with gifts, then prudently decides not to give away his racing pony. Always beside her on the porch is Log-in-the-Creek, who cannot hold his liquor and does not compete in the men's sports, endlessly playing his harmonica as the girl shells vegetables into the pitcher. His name suggests Log-in-the-Creek's apparent worthlessness, his steadiness, even his sexual potency. Here is the legendary third lover who wins the prize.

He does so in his own way, by ignoring the other two. The great contest of folk tradition begins when David Hogganbeck also "looks at" Herman Basket's sister. The pilot is the tall-tale hero, half horse and half alligator. The description of how at high water he brings the steamboat whistling into the plantation belongs with *Life on*

6. See Harry Warren, "Chickasaw Traditions, Customs, Etc.," *Publications of the Mississippi Historical Society*, VIII (Oxford, Miss., 1903), 543–53. The ritual is described in somewhat more detail in Horatio B. Cushman, *History of the Choctaw, Chickasaw and Natchez Indians* (Greenville, Tex., 1899), 369–70, 498. There is no trace here of a male competition for the woman's hand. She not only knew her own mind, as in "A Courtship," but had immediate opportunity to express it.

the Mississippi and Constance Rourke's vignettes of frontier America.

> Then all the People . . . would stand on the landing, to watch the upstairs and the smokestack moving among the trees and hear the puffing of the smokestack and its feet walking fast in the water too when it was not crying. Then we would begin to hear David Hogganbeck's fiddle, and then the steamboat would come walking up the last of the river like a race-horse, with the smoke rolling black and its feet flinging the water aside as a running horse flings dirt, and Captain Studenmare who owned the steamboat chewing tobacco in one window and David Hogganbeck playing his fiddle in the other, and between them the head of the boy slave who turned the wheel, who was not much more than half as big as Captain Studenmare and not even a third as big as David Hogganbeck. And all day long the trading would continue, though David Hogganbeck took little part in this. And all night long the dancing would continue, and David Hogganbeck took the biggest part in this. Because he was bigger than any two of the young men put together almost, and although you would not have called him a man built for dancing or running either, it was as if that very double size which could hold twice as much whiskey as any other, could also dance twice as long, until one by one the young men fell away and only he was left. And there was horse-racing and eating, and although David Hogganbeck had no horses and did not ride one since no horse could have carried him and run fast too, he would eat a match each year for money against any two of the young men whom the People picked, and David Hogganbeck always won.

The puffing smokestack and crying steam whistle; the racehorse metaphor; the triptych of captain, slave, and pilot—build up to the dealing and the dancing, to the hero of a size to match the land and an energy equal to this period when, as W. J. Cash says, "whirl was king." [7] That David Hogganbeck is Boon Hogganbeck's grandfather shows the continuity and distance from the Indian stories to "The Bear." [8]

The description of the pilot's arrival is the curtain-raiser for a stupendous series of events, including a mock-epic eating contest and a footrace of 130 miles. It begins modestly enough, when Ikkemotubbe and David Hogganbeck, driven off Herman Basket's gallery for the night, walk each other home, first to the steamboat and then to Ikkemotubbe's house, and then race back and forth and collapse in Ikkemotubbe's bed. The next night this is repeated and they sleep together in the steamboat (ostensibly to ensure that neither sleeps with the girl). Here is another Faulknerian puberty rite, a substitute for sex. The experience of brotherhood is intensified by racial difference. One recalls the boyhood intimacy between whites and blacks in *The Unvanquished* and "The Fire and the Hearth," which includes sharing the same pallet, and ends when the white boy awakes to the color bar. Roth Edmonds is seven when "the old curse . . . descended to him. . . . So he entered into his heritage. He ate its bitter fruit." In the Arcadian world of "A Courtship" there are Indians instead of blacks, with half-white names, at that, and Faulkner's men are boys again, know-

7. W. J. Cash, *The Mind of the South* (New York, 1954), 25.

8. Asked at Virginia about David Hogganbeck's relationship to Boon, Faulkner replied, "1812 to—yes, that would be Boon's grandfather." See Frederick Gwynn and Joseph L. Blotner (eds.), *Faulkner in the University: Class Conferences in the University of Virginia, 1957–58* (Charlottesville, Va., 1959), 261. The flexible genealogy does not keep him from giving the story a historical date.

ing neither grief nor shame. The extravagance of the competition reflects this imaginative release.

He presents the backwoods equivalents of medieval trials, in an ascending order of severity. The drinking contest is burlesque. After round one Ikkemotubbe rides by the gallery on the whiskey-trader's buckboard wearing the general's coat which General Jackson had given his uncle, "with his arms folded and one foot advanced onto Log-in-the-Creek's back." At the end of the second day, however, "David Hogganbeck was driving the buckboard while the legs of Ikkemotubbe and the other young men dangled from the open door of the little whiskey-house like so many strands of vine hay and Issetibbeha's general coat was tied by its sleeves around the neck of one of the mules." The young men dangling like vine hay and the general's coat around the mule are characteristic of the extravagant but delicately handled humor of "A Courtship." The absurdities of puberty are seen on an exotic stage.

The Indian, of course, loses the eating contest too, for which they starve themselves for a day and a night. He gets through the stewed bird chitterlings and twenty-three turkey eggs, as many as his years, followed by the tongue, paws, and melt of a bear, but the roasted shote is too much for him. The boasting or "tall talk" of the old southwest sets off the fellow-feeling of the men. But when Ikkemotubbe admits he is beaten and Hogganbeck gives him another chance, we are far from the world of Longstreet's "The Fight." The frontier is another age of chivalry. The narrator says that his father told him "how they loved David Hogganbeck at that moment as they loved Ikkemotubbe . . . because there were men in those days." So the tough-minded Lucas Beauchamp sees the time of his white grandfather, Carothers McCaslin, as one "when men black and white were men." The dream of racial equality fuels Faulkner's nostalgias.

The friends resolve upon an ultimate test of strength. They will run to the cave, a hole in the hill over in the country of old David Colbert, a fearful place because the roof is about to fall in. The first to enter fires his pistol up and, if he comes out, wins the girl. Each expects to be killed and save the other, in the best traditions of blood brotherhood. The contestants exhibit the Faulknerian catalogue of love and honor and pity and pride and compassion and sacrifice, and the endurance he values most. They symbolically consummate their courtship at the cave, even as Herman Basket's sister is marrying Log-in-the-Creek.

The three-day marathon is a sentimentalized Greek frieze, Ikkemotubbe leading, describing the landmarks, and in the prairies running "with his hand lying lightly on David Hogganbeck's shoulder, not on top of the shoulder but lightly against the back of it until after a while he would smile at David Hogganbeck and draw ahead." As a Fiedlerite could cite the homoerotic feeling here, so biographical criticism suggests that Faulkner used his memories of the hare and hound games recalled by Calvin Brown, games in which the contestants divided up two or three on a side. The Indian's speed wins him the protective role in the relationship. He slows till David can follow him at night and, when the latter falls, finds him water and food, waiting ahead till his friend can go on. This is not the competitive view of the race of life, in which as Kipling said, "he travels the fastest who travels alone." The slave in "Red Leaves" runs for his life alone, as does Joe Christmas, but both know they will lose, while the men in "A Courtship" survive.

Mr. Brown describes the feeling in their games "of having gone to the limits of endurance and beyond." [9] Faulkner evokes the detachment of exhaustion through Ikkemotubbe, in a style which shows Hemingway's influence: "Then it was sunset again, and then it was dark again, and he lay there listening to David Hogganbeck coming for a long time until it was time for Ikkemotubbe to get up and he did and they went on slowly in the dark with David Hogganbeck at least a hundred paces behind him, until he heard David Hogganbeck fall and he lay down too." It is Hemingway made to serve an openly heroic, epic code, more like *The Old Man and the Sea* than anything Faulkner could have read in 1943. The repetition of the names impresses the characters upon us, especially when the tale is read aloud. "In the four paragraphs which recount the race," a reader notes, "the author repeats the name Ikkemotubbe eighteen times and that of David Hogganbeck thirty-nine times," until they "seem as familiar, as natural, and almost as significant as Agamemnon or Diomedes." [10]

The climax is a tall tale with concessions to modernity and Freud. The capitalization of the word *Cave*, based on the Indian animism, invites symbolic reading. It suggests the return to the womb and second birth; it correlates heterosexual initiation with the fear of death, as this strengthens the male instinct to get out alive.[11] The

9. Calvin S. Brown, "Faulkner's Manhunts: Fact into Fiction," *Georgia Review*, XX (Winter, 1966), 392.

10. Frank Cantrell, "Faulkner's 'A Courtship,'" *Mississippi Quarterly*, XXIV (Summer, 1971), 293.

11. "The Cave is, of course, a great deal more than just a cave," writes

extravagance of the scene does not obscure its implications. Ikkemotubbe runs into the cave and fires his pistol, but Hogganbeck follows him and supports the falling roof with his back. He commands the Indian to crawl out between his legs, and the latter runs back with a pole to take some of the weight. Now, apparently, neither can move. But in an act as practical as it is symbolic Ikkemotubbe, with his back and legs under the pole, "reached one hand and grasped David Hogganbeck by the meat and jerked him backward out of the hole"; after which, miraculously, "it was the pole and not his back which snapped and flung him face-down too across David Hogganbeck like two flung sticks, and a bright gout of blood jumped out of David Hogganbeck's mouth."

The imagery of male climax and exhaustion is plain. The struggle that began with the rivals running back and forth at night is over, leaving them with no immediate need for Herman Basket's sister. Indeed, the gout of blood as a vivid image of menstruation turns David into the woman even as it underscores the fear of woman below the surface of the narrative. The rest is epilogue, a reduction of the world of romance to comedy and the heroes to normal size. Ikkemotubbe, having run a mere forty miles back before he meets the narrator's father with help, is told that there is news. We do not hear it with him, nor is Herman Basket's sister mentioned again by this name. She is referred to but twice, first in the

---

John L. Longley, Jr., in a brief discussion of "A Courtship" in *The Tragic Mask: A Study of Faulkner's Heroes* (Chapel Hill, N.C., 1963), 122, 123. "Entering the Cave, especially with such a deadly purpose, is a descent, a plunge back into the irrational and deadly abyss of the prehuman darkness before man's struggle to create such concepts as justice, chivalry, and reverence for human life." Is Faulkner's Cave *this much* more than just a cave?

people's memory of the scene on the gallery, when, sur-
rounded by her courtiers, "Log-in-the-Creek's wife" had
shelled corn or peas into the wine pitcher. The second
time is when the steamboat carrying the two men out of
the plantation passes "the house where Log-in-the-Creek
and his wife lived," Ikkemotubbe drawing on the "crying-
rope" while Hogganbeck worries about losing steam and
they share the consolations of philosophy.

For all men there is one wisdom, at least one heart-
break, they agree in the perfunctory last paragraphs. It is
a bathetic version of what Tocqueville called a premise
of democratic literature. Male naïveté is underscored. A
mournful Ikkemotubbe recalls a saying that "a woman's
fancy is like a butterfly which, hovering from flower to
flower, pauses at last as like as not where a horse has
stood." Neither man grasps that Log-in-the-Creek has his
own sexual potency—the confidence of his harmonica on
the porch has receded from their consciousness—and that
the girl has made a good choice. In this remote, ostensibly male-dominated American wilderness where she
goes by her brother's name, she has gone her way and
left heroic masculinity without its *raison d'être*. Faulkner's sense of the eternal feminine owes little to the butterfly, a good deal to a sign in red paint which hung over
his mother's kitchen stove, reading *Don't Explain—Don't
Complain*.[12]

He imposes his version of the battle of the sexes, in
which men, suffering from the malady of the ideal, become figures of fun. Their inability to cope, as women
can, regularly qualifies his choice of a man's world. One
thinks of Mrs. Littlejohn when the men are throwing

12. Murry Falkner, *The Falkners of Mississippi* (Baton Rouge, 1967),
9–10.

their money away in *The Hamlet*, at her work and then calmly breaking her washboard over the crazed pony's nose. The matriarchal aspects of many Indian societies, including the southern tribes, support the plot of "A Courtship." Chickasaw women could own property under tribal law when white women in Mississippi could not.[13] Herman Basket's sister's independence also reflects the power of women through the nature which transcends societies.

The tale owes something to the new woman of Faulkner's youth in the 1920s, and to his unsuccessful courtship of Estelle Oldham, whose first marriage was to another man. In their childhood days, John Faulkner writes, "Bill tried to attract her attention by being the loudest one, the daringest. But the more he tried the more mussed he got, and sweatier, and dirtier, and Estelle simply wasn't interested." At nineteen and twenty, however, he was going steady with her, had a job in his grandfather's bank, and was, his brother says, a happy man with limited ambitions. "His world went to pieces" after her engagement to Cornell Franklin: he gave up drawing forever, went north to live briefly with Phil Stone at Yale, and after her June wedding enlisted in the R.A.F.[14] Ikkemotubbe's departure for Natchez and New Orleans, to return seven years later as Doom, is another such sad tale, sweetened by the nostalgic final tableau of the steamboat disappearing around the bend: "That's how it was in the old days."

13. Ward L. Miner, *The World of William Faulkner* (New York, 1952), 21. Miner asserts that the Chickasaw example influenced the Mississippi legislature to pass "a law granting separate property rights to all free married women of the state," in 1839, when such laws were rare indeed in the United States. Faulkner's use of Indian life in "A Courtship" was in this sense historical.

14. John Faulkner, *My Brother Bill: An Affectionate Reminiscence* (New York, 1963), 85, 130, 133.

If Faulkner draws on personal experience, he has the historical situation of the tribe in view. Ikkemotubbe's personal disillusionment is linked with a great leap forward into white culture. He departs in the steamboat—in "A Justice," he is determined to acquire one of his own and does—with Hogganbeck, whom the People trust, but brings home with him a renegade French aristocrat "whom no man wished to love," and brings the instruments of progress: poison, through which to take power, and more slaves than the Indian economy can absorb. "A Justice" shows that Doom is uncorrupted by his tools, but "Red Leaves" portrays the decadence which follows. The quasi-noble savage vanishes under the weight of slavery. In like manner the wilderness was lost, and southern society emerged.

The equilibrium of "A Courtship" seems to owe something to the tribal inertia embodied by the successful Log-in-the-Creek. Faulkner makes an interesting point about sex and race, although it is not Fiedler's point. In the real world the relationship of Ikkemotubbe and Hogganbeck implies an upward mobility from which the Chickasaws have much to lose. In the meantime we enjoy a moment of equality, a moment before the Indians are absorbed into the life Faulkner knew, where race was not so easily exorcised. He identifies this moment imaginatively with his own boyhood Arcadia, to which he knows he can't go home again. Together "Lo!" and "A Courtship" confront an ideal brotherhood with a fact of conflict and imminent dispossession. Neither story attempts to establish the same kind of reality as those which show the impact of slavery upon the tribes, for Faulkner a subject more compelling than the dispossession itself. When Ikkemotubbe leaves on the steamboat, the writer has preceded him.

V ✍ "A Justice"

In "A Justice" the relations of red and white men give way to those of red and black, and the Indian stage becomes a realistic one. Faulkner represents not brotherhood but a crude equality before the law. His tableau is not softened by distance and a rosy light, but set directly before us, along with its interpreter, Sam Fathers. Slapstick and saga meet in Sam's tale, Gothic effects give way to awareness of a black man's rights. The storyteller is recounting his own origins, and a gravely elegiac description of the man enables us to share the effect upon the Faulkner-Quentin listener, aged twelve. A classic in the adaptation of spoken narrative to print, "A Justice" is one of Faulkner's great stories.

Its place in his work is significant. It introduces Sam Fathers and Doom within a Compson family idyll based on the Falkners' Sunday excursions to grandfather's farm. Linking *The Sound and the Fury* and *Go Down, Moses* through their roots in the writer's youth, it is also the heart of his Indian cycle. With "Red Leaves" it prepares for the portraits of blacks in "The Fire and the Hearth" and "Pantaloon in Black." Yet the story goes unmentioned in a checklist of Faulkner criticism forty-five pages long, including scores of entries for the minor novels and something on the most ephemeral of the stories. It is only beginning to be noticed in the 1970s.[1]

With John Faulkner's vignette of their boyhood visits to the farm in mind, one sees how his brother shaped his memories into the backdrop of Sam Fathers' tale. "Until Grandfather Compson died we would go out to the farm every Saturday afternoon," he begins, locating in the lost world of childhood the continuity with the past and relation to the land which the oral tradition assumes. Place is intimately, casually possessed. "This was in North Mississippi," where the hills are steep, because even with "the best team in the county," from their places in the front of the surrey "Roskus and I could smell Grandfather's cigar." [2] Father and mother, part of the Falkner family expeditions, are omitted in this vision of the old order, and there are no tensions between Caddy, Jason, and the narrator. Here is the innocence hungered for in "That Evening Sun" and *The Sound and the Fury.*

The figure of Grandfather prepares the reader for that of Sam Fathers. "A clever carpenter from the quarters,"

1. Maurice Beebe, "Criticism of William Faulkner: A Selected Checklist," *Modern Fiction Studies,* XIII (Spring, 1967), 115–61. The first criticism of the story was Elmo Howell's "Sam Fathers: A Note on Faulkner's 'A Justice,'" *Tennessee Studies in Language and Literature,* XII (1967), 149–53, followed by pp. 271–78 of A. P. Libby's "Chronicles of Children: Faulkner's Short Fiction" (Phd. dissertation, Stanford University, 1969). The most recent is M. E. Bradford's essay, "That Other Patriarchy: Observations on Faulkner's 'A Justice,'" in Bradford's *Of Pride and Humility: Studies in Faulkner's Short Fiction* (Dallas, 1973).

2. Cf. John Faulkner, *My Brother Bill: An Affectionate Reminiscence* (New York, 1963), 72. "I can remember the hazy blue of the hills as they unfolded on our way home and scrounging down behind the front seat where Grandfather and a Negro sat, and smelling the spicy apples, glad we were going home because it was getting dark." William Faulkner's "If there be grief" suggests the same experience: "For where is any death/ While in these blue hills slumbrous overhead/I'm rooted like a tree?" The understatement of "A Justice" effectively establishes the unity of man and land both brothers felt.

he is "a clever negro carpenter" in the manuscript of the story, where the name Sam Fathers seems an afterthought, appearing in the margin before becoming part of the text.[3] Faulkner may not have known his friend's full name. He is introduced as keeping both the farmhouse and the quarters "whole and sound," and the phrase is repeated. One thinks of his fellow carpenters Cash Bundren and Isaac McCaslin, of Faulkner's carpentry metaphors for the writer's art. Such is the storyteller's importance in the social order. Sam's "I remember" impresses itself upon the boy; his "Listen" is authoritative. "Almost a hundred years old," a composite of the two races submerged through the white man's ascendancy, he puts the eldest son, aspiring to manhood, in touch with a past deeper than the family's.

The boy sees both features and manner distinguishing him from the blacks. But he is less pronouncedly Indian than in "The Old People," where he is known as Ikke-motubbe's son, where his mother is not black but a quadroon. In "A Justice" he has kinky hair. His bearing marks him as the survivor of a vanished world: "He was straight in the back, not tall, a little broad, and his face was still all the time, like he might be somewhere else all the while he was working or when people, even white people, talked to him, or while he talked to me. It was just the same all the time, like he might be away up on a roof by himself, driving nails." His opening statement of his origins has authority. He rejects the identities imposed by white men and black. His mammy was black, he was born an Indian, his name was Had-Two-Fathers.

In this scene Sam Fathers, like the boy listener, uses

3. Manuscript of "A Justice," (MS in William Faulkner Collection, Alderman Library, University of Virginia), 1.

the word *nigger*, as he would have in Faulkner's boyhood and in 1931, when "A Justice" appeared. Readers thereby prepared for a racist document will be surprised that within Sam's tale the term is "black people" and the thrust is toward racial justice. He tells of his Indian father's pursuit of his mother, and for all his sense of Indian identity the story sides with her black husband. The plot works around to the chief's defense of black rights—a point is being made to the white boy—and the tale ends on a note of black pride, appropriate if Faulkner heard some of it from a man three-quarters black. The subject of slavery among the Indians is interwoven with the larger legend of Faulkner's tribe and chief.

The chief is Doom, who emerges from the chrysalis of "A Courtship" to dominate "A Justice" and overshadow "Red Leaves" as well. He is a tyrant on the Elizabethan scale. When he returns from New Orleans after the biblical seven years, bringing six slaves won at the gambling table, he also brings "a gold box of New Orleans salt about the size of a gold watch"; a box of puppies on whom to show the effects of this strange salt; and the new name given him "by a French chief," meaning, he says, "the Man." How Doom comes to be the Man, adds the steamboat to his house, and responds to his old companion Craw-ford's interest in the slave woman are interwoven strands of the narrative. It begins as dark comedy, burlesque melodrama, while the steamboat scene is the Faulknerian equivalent of Cecil B. De Mille. The humor acquires a serious point through the racial triangle, Craw-ford, otherwise called "pappy," being a scapegrace villain. The conclusion is Sam Fathers' birth and the revenge of Doom and the black man.

All this is to take the tale at face value, to resist any

temptation to impose the relationships of *Go Down, Moses*, where the whole Indian genealogy is different. The first pieces on "A Justice" do just this, insisting that Sam Fathers is already Doom's son, the black woman his paramour; that Craw-ford is his cover and the chief's 'justice' a cynical parody, an introduction to the moral horror of Yoknapatawpha.[4] Little evidence is suggested for this theory, which ignores Faulkner's plot. Craw-ford is not such a witless stooge as to accept persecution by Doom for the latter's sins, nor would Doom need a dangerous charade to return his mistress to her husband. Behind such readings are frustration with the episodic nature of "A Justice" and its range of tone. Faulkner turns a Machiavel into a benevolent paternalist, and enjoys the conflict over the woman while identifying with the black underdog. For the flexibility of the oral tradition these critics would substitute a mechanical unity.

Doom's name indicates the imaginative unity possessed by the Indian legend. Its derivation from "the Man" shows Faulkner's use of black tradition, while the ostensibly French source, *du homme*, sounds the note of man's fate, in both "A Justice" and the appendix of *The Sound and the Fury*. There the missing step of "called *l'Homme* (and sometimes *de l'homme*)" was inserted on Cowley's advice—Faulkner had ignored the grammatical problem.[5]

4. See Elmo Howell, in *Tennessee Studies in Language and Literature*, XII (1967), 149–53, and Bradford's essay in *Of Pride and Humility: Studies in Faulkner's Short Fiction* (Dallas, 1973). "Sam Fathers, who tells the story to Quentin Compson, has full knowledge of the facts of his birth, but because of his Indian proclivity to secrecy he keeps up the deception even when there is no occasion for doing so," Howell writes (149–59). For Bradford, Sam is Doom's son "as we learn from the naming (a father's prerogative), from his admiration for the child, and from *Go Down, Moses*."

5. Faulkner accepted the change, remarking that he had thought it "righter that Ikkemotubbe, knowing little of French or English either,

He chose the word for its old English meaning too. In "A Justice" the chief "dooms" or judges the tribe, and Faulkner called his projected final survey of his world "the Doomsday Book of Yoknapatawpha County." [6] The name anticipates Ikkemotubbe's role in southern destiny, as the man who deeds Sutpen, McCaslin, and Compson their lands. The ramifications of the theme go on. "Red Leaves" could have been entitled "Doom."

Faulkner could not, however, have persuaded us that the Doom of "A Justice" is the beau ideal of "A Courtship" come of age. Instead we are told that his friends feared him as a boy, that the Man saw in him Cassius' lean and hungry look. "O Sister's Son, your eye is a bad eye, like the eye of a bad horse," the Man would say. The "bad Indian" of popular culture is turned into a hero-villain. On leaving home Ikkemotubbe first renames himself for the steamboat pilot, here called Callicoat rather than Hogganbeck, from the Buster Callicot who worked for Faulkner's father and from whom Boon was partly drawn. "You haven't heard maybe of a David Callicoat getting drowned in the Big River, or killed in the white man's fight in New Orleans?" the Man would fearfully ask the whiskey-trader each summer.[7]

Rule descended in the female line among the Chicka-

should have an easy transition to the apt name he gave himself in English, than that the French should be consistent." Malcolm Cowley, *The Faulkner-Cowley File: Letters and Memories, 1944–1962* (New York, 1966), 42–43.

6. "Interview with Jean Stein vanden Heuvel," in James B. Meriwether and Michael Millgate (eds.), *Lion in the Garden: Interviews with William Faulkner, 1926–1962* (New York, 1968), 255. See also James B. Meriwether, "The Novel Faulkner Never Wrote," *American Literature*, XLII (March, 1970), 93–96.

7. In the crossed-out opening paragraphs of the manuscript of "A Justice" (at Alderman Library, University of Virginia) Doom wants to go to New Orleans when he hears from the whiskey-trader how the white

saws and the Choctaws.[8] This would account for the chief's fear, for the youth would have been his heir, and it is an argument for a source in folk history. But Faulkner's own culture and the figures of Grandfather and Sam Fathers dictate a patrilineal descent, complicating the usurper's task. Doom and his creator are a match for this. In the graphic scene of his return, by the time his friends have reminded him that he is "only on the Sister's side" and the Man has a brother and a son, they have seen the shape of the future:

> Herman Basket told how Doom took a puppy out of the box in which something was alive, and how he made a bullet of bread and a pinch of the salt in the gold box, and put the bullet into the puppy and the puppy died.
>
> . . . .
>
> He said they stood there in the dark, with the other puppies in the box, the ones that Doom hadn't used, whimpering and scuffling, and the light of the pine knot shining on the eyeballs of the black people and on Doom's gold coat and on the puppy that had died.

Its visual intensity makes the bizarre scene real, as the deadpan narration does what follows. With the efficiency of Richard III, Doom engages Herman Basket and Crawford through promises he will not be bound by; frightens the Man's brother, Sometimes-Wakeup, still further into passivity; and poisons the Man and his son.

Faulkner simultaneously begins the serio-comic plot

---

people fight there. This may be closer to what Faulkner heard as a boy than the new beginning with Doom's return from New Orleans to usurp the chieftainship.

8. Arrell M. Gibson, *The Chickasaws* (Norman, Okla., 1971), 19; Angie Debo, *The Rise and Fall of the Choctaw Republic* (Norman, Okla., 1934), 15.

involving pappy, a frustrated Indian paramour, and the black people. Doom offers the six slaves to his two friends, but they decline the gift, since "they already had more black people in the Plantation than they could find use for." It is still a wilderness economy. Their lack of interest is emphatic, and when Craw-ford sees that one of the six is a woman Doom, being Doom, will not let him change his mind. In a slapstick sequence perhaps inspired by Lear's loss of his knights the Indian is reduced from asking for half the slaves, the half with the woman in it, to two including the woman, to the woman only, and denied each time. Promised that he will have her when Doom is chief, he is barely able to contain himself, and when he comes to redeem the promise sooner than he should have, the reply is "What woman?" Their exchange will become a refrain:

" 'I think you don't trust me,' Doom said. . . .

'I think you still believe that puppy was sick.'

Herman Basket said that pappy thought. . . . 'I think it was a well dog,' pappy said."

Doom has no concern for the black husband yet, no motive other than establishing absolute power. The broad humor of his repeated advice to "trust me"—in the extremity of his frustration pappy feels obliged to protest that he does—reminds us that the tale appeared at the end of the Al Capone era. Faulkner can absorb Chicago gangster talk, too.

Behind this are the threat and counterthreat and the bargaining routines of southwestern humor. They color the dialogue of "A Justice," and much of the story is dialogue, a terse, repetitive banter which renders life as well as speech. The beginning of the steamboat episode is typical:

The steamboat was lying on its side on the sand-bar. When they came to it, there were three white men on it. "Now we can go back home," pappy said.

But Doom talked to the white men. "Does this steamboat belong to you?" Doom said.

"It does not belong to you," the white men said. And though they had guns, Herman Basket said they did not look like men who would own a boat.

"Shall we kill them?" he said to Doom. But he said that Doom was still talking to the men on the steamboat.

"What will you take for it?" Doom said.

"What will you give for it?" the white man said.

"It is dead," Doom said. "It's not worth much."

"Will you give ten black people?" the white men said.

"All right," Doom said. "let the black people who came with me from the Big River come forward."

"Horror, terror, death were written large in the life of the rivers and forests," Constance Rourke says.[9] Although Doom would rather trade the slaves than kill the men on the boat, he does not protest when Craw-ford and Herman Basket, to recover the black woman, "fill the white men with rocks and sink them in the river," an incident handled offstage with classical discretion. " 'The white men went away, did they?' Doom said. 'So it seems,' pappy said." Others can play this ruthless game. Craw-ford tries to separate the woman from her husband, asking him whether he wants "to be arranged in the river with rocks in your inside too?" " 'Do you want to be arranged in the river yourself?' the black man said to pappy. 'There are two of you, and nine of us." The brotherhood of "A Courtship" gives way to a tougher version of frontier democracy.

9. Constance Rourke, *American Humor: A Study of the National Character* (New York, 1953), 40.

The moving of the steamboat illustrates Faulkner's fusion of humor and saga. "It just seemed to me an awfully good story," he said of the chief hunting the People through the woods with dogs and making them and the slaves drag the boat the twelve miles to the plantation.[10] It is the comic analogue of the creation of the southern mansion in *Absalom, Absalom,* and Doom's implacable will anticipates Sutpen's. The author makes good use of his reading. There is a droll echo, via the Indian animism, of the raising of Lazarus—" 'Now,' Doom said, 'let us make the steamboat get up and walk.' " As he presides from the foredeck the chief recalls both Tamburlaine's "Holla, ye pampered jades of Asia! What! can ye draw but twenty miles a day," and Cleopatra on her barge. "Doom sat in his chair with a boy with a branch to shade him and another boy with a branch to drive away the flying beasts. The dogs rode on the boat too." [11] These glimpses of the will to power in the Mississippi swamps suggest the self-image of the "sole owner and proprietor" of Yoknapatawpha. Faulkner once commissioned his brother John, who painted, to do the scene as a mural for his study.[12]

They are five months getting the steamboat out of the

10. "Interview with Henry Nash Smith," in Meriwether and Millgate (eds.), *Lion in the Garden,* 31.

11. Faulkner often spoke of Shakespeare, whereas his love for Marlowe —shared by other writers of the twenties, including Dos Passos—is less well known. In Japan he said he preferred Marlowe's poetry to Shakespeare's ("Interviews in Japan," in Meriwether and Millgate [eds.], *Lion in the Garden,* 119); and he once coupled Marlowe's plays with the *Tentation de Sainte Antoine* and the Old Testament as his measure of success ("Interview with Cynthia Grenier," *ibid.* 235–36).

12. John Faulkner, *My Brother Bill,* 175. Faulkner's brother wrongly remembers the scene as from "Red Leaves." That he did not know these stories well helps substantiate the authenticity of his memories of their childhood visits to the farm.

river bottom, cutting down cypress trees to make a path for it, another two months using the logs as rollers. A special place is reserved for pappy on a rope just in front of Doom's chair. He invites his scapegoat role by never playing fair with his black rival. On the excuse of a sore back he manages to spend three days courting the woman, with results the reader can foresee. But Doom stops this by suggesting that, to get well sooner, he "sit in the Spring at night too," with one of the black people to keep the fire going. (" 'Which one of the black people?' pappy said. 'The husband of the woman which I won on the steamboat,' Doom said. 'I think my back is better,' pappy said.") That Doom is in control lets us enjoy the rogue while identifying with the black underdog.

The struggle between the two incorporates a uniquely Faulknerian use of southwestern gambling tales, comparable to the poker game over Miss Sophonsiba's marriage which opens *Go Down, Moses*. Pappy proposes to settle their dispute by a cockfight. The black has no cock, and the Indian first calls this a default and claims the woman, setting the ground rules with the logic of the privileged. Of course he finds Doom's champion cock opposite his in the pit, a gift to his opponent. He sacrifices his bird after extracting the husband's consent that it doesn't settle things, and the latter jumps up and down on the dead cock in frustration and rage.

The symbolic suggestiveness of the word "cock" is appropriate. Identifying with the black against the sexual predator, Faulkner obliquely speaks truths about the South on his Indian stage. He expresses the white man's repressed consciousness, as in the dream of innocent brotherhood in "A Courtship." There the Indians are in a sense surrogate blacks, whereas they are surrogate

whites in "Red Leaves" and "A Justice." The black husband's last indignity is the birth to his wife of the "fine
yellow man" whom Doom names Had-Two-Fathers.
When he asks for justice, the practical reply is that justice won't darken the child.

In the humorous resolution racial equality emerges
from male solidarity, as in "A Courtship." "Any man is
entitled to have his melon patch protected from these
wild bucks of the woods," the chief says and orders the
building of a fence around the man's cabin. The Indian
is confronted with a sapling high across two posts:

" 'Climb this fence, and I will give you the woman,'
Doom said.

Herman Basket said pappy looked at the fence awhile.
'Let me go under this fence,' he said.

. . . .

'We will build the fence this high,' Doom said."
Like the Mikado he makes the punishment fit the crime.
The climactic episode is a fine tall tale. The squat Indian, who "can't build a fence I couldn't climb," has to
build one that the black can sail over like a bird, taking
the better part of a year to do it, dragging the saplings in
from the creek bottom by hand because Doom will not
let him use the wagon. He finishes as his antagonist holds
a second baby up from inside and asks, "What do you
think about this for color?" Pappy sees that, in Huckleberry Finn's words, "overreachin' don't pay."

The authority of the Man makes plausible the fair
treatment of the slave. Doom's progress from "bad" Indian to enlightened despot has been rapid, but his mo-
tives are not sentimentalized. He does not consult the
woman, whose preference remains unclear. If he acknowledges the sexual rights of man, he also resembles

the Tudor monarch who took the commoner's side to keep the barons down. But is the outcome true to the Indians' relations with their slaves? It is a counterimage to the vulnerability of the black woman on the white plantation, source of the moral horror of "The Bear". Is the image broadly historical?

From the black accounts, at any rate, Indian masters respected the slave's manhood. As Faulkner does, these accounts stress the lack of an intensive market agriculture, the man-to-man relations of the races, the integrity of the black family. Henry Bibb, author of one of the slave narratives, belonged briefly to a Cherokee, to whom he was sold by gamblers, as Doom acquired the slaves in "A Justice." "My master," he writes, "was the owner of a large plantation and quite a number of slaves. He raised corn and wheat for his own consumption only. There was no cotton, tobacco, or anything of the kind produced among them for the market." Bibb contrasts his experience of "negro slavery among the Indians, and the same thing among the white slave-holders of the South":

> The Indians allow their slaves enough to eat and wear. They have no overseers to whip nor drive them. If a slave offends his master, he sometimes, in a heat of passion, undertakes to chastize him, but it is as often the case as otherwise that the slave gets the better of the fight, and even flogs his master, for which there is no law to punish him; but when the fight is over that is the last of it. So far as religious instruction is concerned, they have it on terms of equality, the bond and the free; they have no respect of persons, they have neither slave pews nor negro pews. Neither do they separate husbands and wives, nor parents and children.[13]

13. From the *Narrative of the Life and Adventures of Henry Bibb Written by Himself* (1849), in Ruth Miller (ed.), *Blackamerican Literature* (Beverly Hills, Calif., 1971), 109.

Thus the People and the black people tow the steamboat and watch the cockfight side-by-side, and they are equally on the husband's side against Craw-ford. Bibb does not idealize the Indians, complaining of their drunkenness, dirtiness, their "savage and unChristian practices." He would recognize the violence of Faulkner's scene. But the relative equality and justice he describes seem utopian by contrast with the great plantations of the deep South.

The memories of an ex-slave in the Indian Territory fill out the picture. Mary Grayson's master was a full-blooded Creek, in the part of the Territory where the Creeks sided with the South in the Civil War. "All the Negroes I knew who belonged to Creeks," she says, "always had plenty of clothes and lots to eat, and we all lived in good log cabins we built. We worked the farm and tended to the horses and cattle and hogs, and some of the women worked around the owner's house, but each Negro family looked after a part of the fields and worked the crops like they belonged to us." [14] She also has her criticisms of the Indians. One finds the full force of black romanticization of the red men in the black writer Martin Delany, for whom they are chivalrous allies in the coming war against the oppressor. In *Blake: or The Huts of America* Delany has a Choctaw chief boast of the egalitarianism of Indian slavery and urge complete intermarriage with the blacks, on the Seminole mode—this in 1859, when the Choctaws were about to ally themselves with the Confederacy.[15] The reports from personal experience are much closer to Faulkner's tale than to this.

Faulkner, however, also softens history. Missing in "A Justice" is the most obvious motive the chief would have

14. "Mary Grayson: Indian Territory," *Lay My Burden Down: A Folk History of Slavery*, ed. B. A. Botkin (Chicago, 1945), 131.
15. From Martin R. Delany, *Blake: Or the Huts of America*, in Miller (ed.), *Blackamerican Literature*, 200–202.

had in separating Craw-ford and the woman. Delany to the contrary, the Choctaws, Chickasaws, and Cherokees outlawed intermarrying with blacks; and "in 1838 the Choctaw National Council passed a law prohibiting the cohabitation of any member of the nation wth a Negro slave." [16] Lafferty plays this down in his novel of the Choctaws and the Indian Territory, *Okla Hannali*. Apparently the less exclusive of the Creeks were known as "nigger Creeks." As sociologist Edgar Z. Friedenberg has remarked, "Indians, for some reason, are just as racist as anybody else." [17] Faulkner represents this as a later phase of Indian slavery in "Red Leaves," but if the fence in "A Justice" had been built around the black man's home, fair play would probably not have been the first reason, nor would the chief have had Doom's equanimity about the yellow baby.

Sam Fathers naturally sees things this way, in affirming his own mixed blood. The coloration of the tale is further evidence that Faulkner heard something like it from a black with Indian ancestry, a product of the cohabitation the Choctaw council tried to stop. Indian hostility to miscegenation may be implicit in the fact that Doom sold Sam's mother to Quentin's great-grandfather. In "The Old People" the deal, no longer reported to us by Sam, includes the baby boy, who has here become Doom's son! "A Justice" stresses the egalitarian aspect of Indian slavery. The black husband's "What do you think about this for color?" is an appropriate last word. It is

16. Wyatt F. Jeltz, "The Relations of Negroes and Choctaw and Chickasaw Indians," *Journal of Negro History*, XXXIII (January, 1948), 31.

17. Edgar Z. Friedenberg, "Southern Discomfort," *New York Review of Books*, XVII (September 2, 1971), 8.

Faulkner's "black is beautiful," forty years ahead of schedule.

The coda which returns the boy listener to his own world, is not the least of the story's distinctions. It is efficient and modest, yet the moment is intense and the writing pure. Before the last episode we have seen the narrator deliberately relighting his pipe, "rising and lifting between thumb and forefinger from his forge a coal of fire," with the family gathered at the carriage and Grandfather calling the boy's name. Now he answers, "with that immediacy of children with which they flee temporarily something which they do not quite understand"; that, and admiration of Grandfather. The romanticized head of the family sets off the authoritarian Doom, and Sam Fathers mediates between the two. In this sense patriarchy and paternalism center the tale.

Like the boy, the horses move quickly, impatient for home. The sun is down and darkness is coming on. As the curtain closes we glimpse Caddy with one very small fish and "wet to the waist," a poignant reminder of the image from which Faulkner said *The Sound and the Fury* sprang, the little girl with muddy drawers watching her grandmother's funeral from the tree. The concluding passage gains resonance if we know that *The Sound and the Fury* was called "Twilight" in manuscript.[18]

"What were you and Sam talking about?" Grandfather said.

We went on, in that strange, faintly sinister suspension of twilight in which I believed that I could still see Sam

18. Linton Massey, *William Faulkner: "Man Working, 1919–62"* (Charlottesville, Va., 1968), 35. The first page of the holograph manuscript is reproduced on p. 36.

Fathers back there, sitting on his wooden block, definite, immobile, and complete, like something looked upon after a long time in a preservative bath in a museum. That was it. I was just twelve then, and I would have to wait until I had passed on and through and beyond the suspension of twilight. Then I knew that I would know. But then Sam Fathers would be dead.

"Nothing, sir," I said. "We were just talking." [19]

The inevitable question and answer reflect the gulf between youth and age, innocence and knowledge. Sam Fathers' death parallels the reference to Grandfather's in the opening sentence of "A Justice," thus bracketing the protected boyhood world. The passage anticipates the ritual coming of age in "The Old People" and "The Bear", as well as the lost modern world of *The Sound and the Fury*.

Calvin Brown, memorialist of Faulkner's games of hare and hounds, has also written of his use of storytelling as "a formative and beneficent force in the lives of his characters." "A Justice" could serve as the text for Mr. Brown's argument that "a living oral tradition can teach a man—and especially a child—who and what he is, can save him from the agonized and rootless 'search for identity' of so many of the heroes and antiheroes of contemporary fiction." [20] Yet Faulkner's tale is less comforting than the formula. His old order is itself mortal, and the description of Sam Fathers on his wooden block—which suggests Darl's description of Jewel from the same

19. The boy's answer does not exist in the manuscript, which ends with the word *dead*. The last line, which completes the story, came to Faulkner later, as was the case more than once with his stories, some of which went through many drafts.

20. Calvin S. Brown, "Faulkner's Use of the Oral Tradition," *Georgia Review*, XXII (Summer, 1968), 166, 167.

period, "his pale eyes set like wood into his wooden face" —is not that of a guide to life. He is a relic of the past, as remote, finally, as Keats's urn, the alter-inspiration of "The Bear."

The boy now leaves Sam's world for town, where the rough justice of the frontier and the Indian does not obtain. In "That Evening Sun," a companion piece to this story, the children's father cannot provide his servant the protection the savage chief gives his slave. The Indians are subject to corruption too, as the distance from "A Courtship" to "A Justice" shows, and Doom has set in motion the transformation of the domain by slavery recorded in "Red Leaves." The happy ending of Sam's tale is an alternative to a scene of which the writer must have often thought, with the "old justice" of *The Hamlet*, "I can't stand no more! This court's adjourned!"

The Faulkner-Quentin boy of twelve, in all his innocence of what the story means, knows he will only understand his friend when he has lost him. Here he anticipates the young Isaac McCaslin, who knows that the chase of Old Ben is the beginning of the end of something, and that Sam's death will be part of it. Not until he is twenty-one can Ike say, "Sam Fathers set me free." Faulkner's fabulous and entertaining tale concludes on the note of harmonious community. Grandfather acknowledges the importance of the boy's experience when he asks "What were you and Sam talking about?" The answer doubles as a graceful understatement of the merits of "A Justice." " 'Nothing, sir,' I said. 'We were just talking.' "

VI.🐌 "Red Leaves"

I

"Red Leaves," longest and most intense of the tales, is a darker vision of the Indian world and of what it means to be a man. There is no innocence here, no storytelling affirmation, and we behold not a justice but an arbitrary doom, the taking of "the Negro's" life to sustain a tribal ritual, by men whose impassivity strengthens the reader's horror. Faulkner shows the remnants of an archaic culture surviving among and on the terms of the intruding whites. His Chickasaws include Three Basket and Louis Berry, stoical elders of the tribe, and the new chief Moketubbe, whose mound of flesh is the embodiment of Indian decay. The slave's experience evokes both black martyrdom and man's capacity for endurance. The story moves from the begining of his six-day flight to the moment before his burial with his dead master Issetibbeha, alternately portraying the pursuers and the pursued. A local folktale becomes a catharsis of pity and fear.

The story has been called magnificent, marvelous, unquestionably a masterpiece, since the English reviews of Faulkner's first collection, *These Thirteen,* yet it has never received sustained attention. Some of the scattered comments are useful. Irving Howe speaks of "the cycle of flight from and reconciliation to one's fate," the eloquence of Faulkner's narrative voice, "the air of a folk-tale or miniature epic." Alfred Kazin appreciates the characterization of the Indians, with their nostalgia for the days before slavery, their grim humor—"philosophi-cal-minded, yet so detached in their fatalism (the world moves as it must and men must die) that they can insist on their ritual without, as it were, having to respect it." Elmo Howell amplifies Faulkner's comment that the red leaves are the Indians in their inevitable and impersonal destruction of the black. This is a "savage world where man is only another expression of the general amorality of nature," and the tale reflects the joy as well as the horror of life on these terms. In *Faulkner and the Negro* Charles H. Nilon follows the slave's experience, showing how his strength and the weaknesses of the masters imply the survival of one race and the possible extinction of the other.[1]

The unique achievement of "Red Leaves" is clearer by comparison with "Dry September," an equally grim study

1. "It is a magnificent, a marvellous story, a work which only a great creative artist could have written," said David Garnett in *New Statesman and Nation*, VI (September 30, 1933), 387. He saw the story moving from crudest parody to the sublime, and this range of tone is one of its char-acteristics. One finds similar praise in the surveys of Faulkner's stories by Alfred Kazin in *Contemporaries* (Boston, 1962), 156–57, and Irving Howe, *William Faulkner: A Critical Study* (New York, 1952), 267. "Red Leaves" is well known among writers. Reviewing Vance Bourjaily's novel *Brill Among the Ruins* (New York, 1970) in *New York Times Book Review*, November 1, 1970, p. 5, James B. Frakes sees one of its best scenes derivative of Faulkner's tale. William Styron singles out "Red Leaves" in commenting on Cowley's discussion of Faulkner in *A Second Flowering: Works and Days of the Lost Generation*, in *New York Times Book Review*, May 6, 1973, p. 10.

Kazin and Howe are quoted from the passages cited above, Howell from "William Faulkner and the Mississippi Indians," *Georgia Review*, XXI (Fall, 1967), 21, 389. See also Elmo Howell, "William Faulkner's Chickasaw Legacy: A Note on 'Red Leaves,'" *Arizona Quarterly*, XXVI

of racial murder. There Faulkner works with stereotypes
—the lynchers and their victim, the ineffective good man,
the sex-starved old maid and her girl friends. The writer's intense conviction makes them real, and the reader's
response is protest and nausea. The Indian stage allows
for a tragic perspective and more complex characterization. The masters are carrying out a duty to the dead, and
they take no pleasure in the task, unconcerned as they
are on the black's behalf. Their laziness, sense of fair
play, and burgherlike mediocrity relieve and underscore
the horror of the act. The victim, who endured the middle passage and has an African community behind him,
is not the cringing "good nigger" of "Dry September."
He becomes man struggling against the end he knows
will come, while the Indians play a waiting, summoning
role, terrible in their grumbling detachment and their
final insistence.

"Red Leaves" is also a work of humor and satire. At
Virginia, Faulkner said that "there's not too fine a distinction between humor and tragedy, that even tragedy
is in a way walking a tightrope between the ridiculous—
between the bizarre and the terrible." The story is full
of incongruous, absurd detail, from the first description
of Three Basket wearing a snuff box on his ear, to Isse-

(Winter, 1970), 293–303, and Charles H. Nilon, *Faulkner and the Negro*
(New York, 1965), 39–43. At Virginia, Faulkner spoke of the meaning
of the title. "It was the deciduation of nature which no one could stop
that had suffocated, destroyed the Negro. That the red leaves had nothing against him when they suffocated and destroyed him. They had
nothing against him, they probably liked him, but it was normal deciduation which the red leaves, whether they regretted it or not, had nothing
more to say in." Frederick Gwynn and Joseph L. Blotner (eds.), *Faulkner in the University: Class Conferences in the University of Virginia,
1957–58* (Charlottesville, Va., 1959), 39.

tibbeha's Parisian gilt bed hanging from deer thongs in
his house, to the slobbering deaf-mute who guards the
drums of the blacks in the swamp. The Indians' talk sup-
plies a new perspective on slavery. Convinced that the
blacks "like sweating," they blame the slave for putting
them to the trouble of pursuing him. He "would rather
even work in the sun than to enter the earth with a
chief." It is a parody of the master class and its rationale,
a comic vision of a doomed culture. To the fugitive and
the reader are left what Faulkner's Nobel Prize speech
calls "the agony and sweat of the human spirit."

The obscurity of the background helps explain why
the tale has been praised in passing. Most readers cannot
have known how much of this is fantasy. The growth of
slavery among the Chickasaws was not. In one party moving west in the 1840s, six Indians owned 263 slaves, with
the richest owning 95. He was a mixed blood, and it may
be objected that Faulkner assigns the sins of mixed and
largely white Indians to the tribe at large. But Gibson's
new history notes that the attitudes of the owners spread
throughout Chickasaw society, "which, as a microcosm of
the larger American society, generated notions of superi-
ority and a presumed social stratification. . . . The slave
performed labor generally scorned by Indians. . . . Slavery
fed [their] aristocratic pretensions in their drive to imi-
tate white planter neighbors." As Howell says, Faulkner
may have felt some satisfaction in transposing the hated
system from the white South, but he was not false to the
record. An observer of the southern Indians in the 1830s
wrote that "the possession of slaves, by rendering the Indians idle and dependent on slave-labour, has confirmed
the defects of their character." "By 1861," Gibson says,

the Chickasaw Nation was an intensely dedicated slave-holding community." [2]

The adaptation of the atavistic Indian ritual to the plantation scene makes "Red Leaves" grimly bizarre. To the anthropologist it is understandable enough: "While Indians may 'clothe' themselves, so to speak, with many of the accouterments of white man's culture, this is often no more than skin-deep. Even when the Indian has been brought into close contact with the white man for more than a generation, and despite missionary efforts and educational opportunities, there is a psychological lag to be taken into account which indicates a dimension of the acculturation process about which we know too little." [3] Faulkner is less ethnocentric than this, less convinced of the inevitability of assimilation. His Chickasaws wear the white man's clothes in curious ways, and they cannot get their feet into the red slippers Issetibbeha brings back from a trip to Paris paid for by the slave trade. Nonetheless the Parisian slippers become the token of his rule, and Moketubbe, fascinated by them from birth, has apparently poisoned his father to make them his. While pursuing the slave in his litter he alternately wears and carries them in his lap. It is a kind of deracinated totem-

2. The figures are derived from Wyatt F. Jeltz, "The Relations of Negroes and Choctaw and Chickasaw Indians," *Journal of Negro History*, XXXIII (January, 1948), 28. The observer of the tribes in the 1830s is William Kennedy, *Texas, Its Rise, Progress, and Prospects* (2 vols.; London, 1841), I, 150, quoted in Kenneth W. Porter, "Relations Between Negroes and Indians Within the Present Limits of the United States," *Journal of Negro History*, XVII (July, 1932), 327. The other quotations in this paragraph are from Arrell M. Gibson, *The Chickasaws* (Norman, Okla., 1971), 124–25 and 41–42. See also Howell, "Faulkner's Chickasaw Legacy," 294.

3. A. Irving Hallowell, "The Backwash of the Frontier: The Impact of the Indian on American Culture," in Walker D. Wyman and Clifton B. Krober (eds.), *The Frontier in Perspective* (Madison, Wisc., 1957), 234.

ism, a grotesque joke on the nineteenth-century view of the progress of the Five Civilized Tribes.

Gibson's history partly supports this vision. He stresses the corrosive influence of European culture before 1800. "Decay in Chickasaw ways and natural law, corruption of personal and tribal honor, and disintegration of institutions and society were conspicuously evident." Three Basket and Louis Berry confront such a scene in "Red Leaves." The vacuum was filled by the material progress of the next thirty years, when the southern tribes became farmers and traders and operated ferries on the rivers, slowly developing an economy like the white man's. Most of this, like Negro slavery, was managed by and for the mixed bloods, while the full bloods, hard hit by the shrinkage of the hunting range, had little to replace the old ways. Many turned to alcohol—the missionaries were always lamenting the drunkenness of the Chickasaws— and others tried to preserve the old religion. The funerary sacrifice in "Red Leaves" may be seen in this context.[4]

4. Gibson, *The Chickasaws*, 106–21 *passim*. The historian quotes a melancholy missionary report of 1836:

> There was an enduring hard core of conservatives, largely among the full bloods, who were determined to preserve and continue the old tribal ways . . . According to one report, two women who had joined the Tokshish church were "abused by their own unmerciful relatives. One was driven from her house, her persecutors "spoiled all her furniture, beat her off into the woods, and vowed her death" (118). "Under the influence of strong temptation they give themselves up to idleness, gambling, and intoxication; and are of course, disinclined and unfit to listen to instruction. . . . The members of the church amounting, a year ago, to nearly one hundred, have been subjected to a fiery trial. Many give fearful evidence of fatal apostasy" (121).

The consolation of the missionaries, interestingly, was the Indians' slaves, who were "much more receptive to evangelizing than the Indians" (117). About two thirds of the members of one church were blacks who conducted Christian exercises in the Chickasaw language. Faulkner's slaves with their primitive Afro-Indian customs may be less historical than his decaying Indian culture.

Faulkner had heard the story Mrs. Holt published in 1936 apropos the Toby Tubby Creek in northwest Lafayette County: "This little tributary of the Tallahatchie River is named for an old Indian Chief named the Toby who lived here when the treaty [the Pontotoc Creek treaty in 1832, which sent the Chickasaws to Indian Territory] was signed. It is said that he was very wealthy and owned many slaves. When he died, a slave was selected to be buried with him, but some white people heard of the plan and prevented it." [5] If this is something the white people invented, as they used tales of the red men to frighten naughty children, its cruelty is no libel on the Chickasaws, who in 1816 "killed several [Negro] slaves for minor offenses by whipping and burning them." [6] There were Caribbean tribes who took their servants with them to the land of the dead, and the Choctaw funeral drawn on in "The Bear" had included the burial of a dog for companionship and, after the Indians acquired horses, a pony for the spirit to ride. Throughout "Red Leaves" Issetibbeha's horse and dog are tethered at the open grave awaiting the slave's arrival.

Faulkner's primary example was the Natchez. Upon the death of the Natchez chief, called the Great Sun, his wives, guards, and other retainers were elaborately executed. The Great Sun's feet were not allowed to touch the ground; when pursuing the slave, Moketubbe is carried in a litter by relays of bearers. Faulkner may have seen the explorer Du Pratz's drawing of the chief's ceremonial processions. It is often reproduced, and the Frenchman's description of the Natchez quoted or paraphrased,

5. Minnie Smith Holt, "Oxford, Mississippi" (typescript, University of Mississippi Library, 1936), 25. The passage includes a tale of buried treasure which may have contributed to "The Fire and the Hearth."
6. Jeltz, "Relations of Negroes, Choctaw and Chickasaw Indians," 26.

as a source for the probable ceremonial life of the mound builders. A novelist of the Indians speaks of recognizing in a sketch of the mound builders the feeling for a people he had encountered in "Red Leaves." [7] Faulkner probably did not know that when the Natchez were smashed by the French in the early eighteenth century, remnants survived among their Muskogean cousins, including the Chickasaws, and were "looked upon as having mystic powers." [8] Assuming the persistence of the past within the present, and the artist's control of time, he captures something of the high civilization of the American Indian as well as its decline.

He must also have been reading Frazer, whose sacrificial priesthood of the golden bough is filled by a man who can outrun his pursuers, by a slave in the slave-owning societies of the ancient world. Frazer tells how "the life of the god-man is prolonged on condition of his showing, in a severe physical contest of fight or flight, that his bodily strength is not decayed, and that, therefore, the violent death, which sooner or later is inevitable, may for the present be postponed." [9] Faulkner's

7. Frederick Manfred, author of *Lord Grizzly, Conquering Horse, Scarlet Plume,* and a novella, *Arrow of Love,* in a letter to the author, September 22, 1972. Mr. Manfred, who believes that the feel and impact of the reports on the Natchez had somehow reached Faulkner, credits him with a complete evocation of a stone-age mind and culture in "Red Leaves."

8. Robert Silverberg, *Mound Builders of Ancient America* (Greenwich, Conn., 1968), 330. The survival of a few Natchez among the other tribes is also noted in Peter Farb, *Man's Rise to Civilization* (New York, 1968), and a copy of Du Pratz's sketch of the progresses of "Le Grand Soleil" included there.

9. James G. Frazer, *The Golden Bough: A Study in Magic and Religion* (New York, 1952), 349–50. In *"Sanctuary* and Frazer's Slain Kings," *Mississippi Quarterly,* XXIV (Summer, 1971), 151, Thomas L. McHaney shows how the mythology of *The Golden Bough* stands behind the characters and ritual of this novel, and suggests Frazer's importance in Faulkner's work. As McHaney says, Faulkner followed Eliot and Joyce in adapting classical material to his own world partly by parody.

slave postpones it for six days. Frazer also shows how through slavery the ritual gradually lost its force as the victim became not a priest-king but an easily expendable figure.[10] This fit in with Faulkner's idea of the decay of the Indians as holders of black slaves, and it freed him to treat the survival of the archaic as burlesque. The decadent fertility rite—"Dry September" is another such—recurs throughout his work.

Contrasted with the Indians are the blacks, not a few slaves as in "A Justice" but a mass with an apparently intact African tribal life. The Chickasaws have now lost their identity with the wilderness, yet their society is still closer to it than was the white plantation, hence the integrity of the slaves can be preserved and respected. Faulkner turns the quarters into an African village in Mississippi, complete with council house, headman, and religious ceremonies carried out in the creek bottom according to the phases of the moon. Drums beat loudly in the background, and there is a flavor of voodoo in the fetishism of the blacks and snake cult of the chief's servant. The latter wears an amulet made of the skull of a moccasin he has killed and eaten. At the first climax of the tale he is prepared for death by the slashing blows of the moccasin he greets as his grandfather.[11]

10. This thread of Frazer's argument is summarized by Daniel Weiss in "William Faulkner and the Runaway Slave," *Northwest Review*, VI (Summer, 1963), 76. Weiss is concerned with the black as ritual object in "Dry September" and "Was" and does not make the application to "Red Leaves".

11. The description of the amulet in the manuscript of "Red Leaves" shows that Faulkner knew little of primitive ritual when he began the story. He looked this up and worked it out as he went along. The passage reads as follows, with brackets indicating words crossed out as he wrote: "it was one-half of a mother of pearl lorgnon which he wore in a cloth sack with the [bullet which had killed a] dried head of a cotton-mouth moccasin, [since the moccasin was his brother] [because he had a

The black community is associated with the fecund earth and nature. In the council house, silent when questioned about the fugitive, the slaves seem to Basket and Berry "like the roots of a huge tree uncovered, the earth broken momentarily upon the writhen, thick, fetid tangle of its lightless and outraged life." The doomed man sees the vital force of his people more romantically, imagining the ritual dancing "where the women with young children crouched, their heavy, sluggish breasts nippled full and smooth into the mouths of men children; contemplative, oblivious of the drumming." Such passages suggest that Faulkner had encountered the Négritude school of poets and philosophers. He is also a serious Darwinian, and here fuses animist religion with the capacity of the blacks to survive. The virtue he wryly attributes to the species in the Nobel speech he saw embodied in the black American.

Hidden in the barn, hearing the thin whispers of rat feet along the rafters, the slave remembers a time when he had eaten rat:

> He was a boy then, but just come to America. They had lived ninety days in a three-foot-high 'tween-deck in tropic latitudes, hearing from topside the drunken New England captain intoning aloud from a book which he did not recognize for ten years afterward to be the Bible. Squatting in the stable so, he had watched the rat, civilized, by association with man reft of its inherent cunning of limb and eye; he had caught it without difficulty, with scarce a movement of his hand, and he ate it slowly, wondering how

---

reason for the snake's head. He had been told that he would die of a snake] which was his grandfather; he killed the snake himself and ate it save the head" (MS, "Red Leaves," in William Faulkner Collection, Alderman Library, University of Virginia). In revision the description becomes more vivid, while the grandfather is saved for the ritual greeting.

any of the rats had escaped so long. At that time he was still wearing the single white garment which the trader, a deacon in the Unitarian church, had given him, and he spoke then only his native tongue.[12]

That the *man* has escaped so long is cause for wonder. The passage is a tribute like the summing up of Dilsey: "They endured." The failure of the Indians to endure was equally vivid for Faulkner, the contrast sharp. Once, in Japan, he compared the Negro with the Indian. Although the former seemed fated for assimilation into the white race "simply because there are more white people," Faulkner said, "he has a force, a power of his own that will enable him to survive. He won't vanish as the Indian did, because he is stronger and tougher than the Indian." [13] "Red Leaves" shows this even in the slave's defeat and extinction.

II

The story unfolds slowly in the bizarre, compelling Indian scene. The description of Basket and Berry removes us from the present while preparing for a searing action: "Squat men, a little solid, burgherlike; paunchy, with big heads, big, broad, dust-colored faces of a certain blurred serenity like carved heads on a ruined wall in Siam or Sumatra, looming out of a mist. The sun had done it, the violent sun, the violent shade. Their hair looked like sedge grass on burnt-over land." Faulkner shapes the stoicism of the Indians into an insensibility that sets off the black's suffering. He relies heavily on dia-

12. There were and are no deacons in the Unitarian church. Faulkner's attack on the Yankee slavers falls into southern stereotype.
13. "Interviews in Japan," in James B. Meriwether and Michael Millgate (eds.), *Lion in the Garden: Interviews with William Faulkner, 1926–1962* (New York, 1968), 182–83.

logue. This is also true in "A Justice," but the dialogue
of "Red Leaves," lacking the filters of Sam Fathers and
the author-listener, directly creates the mood and tone:

> "Yao. They are nothing but a trouble and a care."
> "Maybe it will not take three days."
> "They run far. Yao. We will smell this Man before he
> enters the earth. You watch and see if I am not right."
> They approached the house.
> "He can wear the shoes now," Berry said. "He can wear
> them now in man's sight."
> "He cannot wear them for a while yet," Basket said.
> Berry looked at him. "He will lead the hunt."
> "Moketubbe?" Berry said. "Do you think he will? A man
> to whom even talking is travail?"
> "What else could he do? It is his own father who will
> soon begin to smell."
> "That is true," Berry said. "There is even yet a price
> he must pay for the shoes. Yao. He has truly bought them.
> What do you think?"
> "What do you think?"
> "What do you think?"
> "I think nothing."
> "Nor do I. Issetibbeha will not need the shoes now. Let
> Moketubbe have them; Issetibbeha will not care."
> "Yao. Man must die."
> "Yao. Let him; there is still the Man."

As in "A Courtship" Hemingway's influence is plain.
The short sentences and repetitions, combining American idiom with a stylized evocation of an older, ceremonial culture, the matter-of-fact and oblique tone, are
adapted to Faulkner's scene in all its fatalism and gro-
tesquerie. He is said to have told one of his editors that
he had difficulty with the dialogue of "Red Leaves" and

solved the problem while rereading *Death in the After-noon*: "The stilted, formalized Castilian-into-English which Hemingway had contrived seemed to Faulkner's ear to have just the right intonation for his Indians, and so his dialogue became a graceful though individualized borrowing—as anyone who compares the two works will readily see." [14] But William Styron, who recounted this, has since acknowledged that Hemingway's salute to bull-fighting appeared two years before "Red Leaves," and in fact the resemblances are not large. "The Undefeated," a bullfight story Faulkner could have read before 1930, parallels his tale in theme; and the title, *The Unvan-quished*, suggests its influence on him. The dialogue in "The Undefeated," however, is no closer to "Red Leaves" than is that in Hemingway's novels. Faulkner's debt re-mains plain and is significant to the study of the two writers. It marks the literary community of a generation, as Styron says.

Before we meet Moketubbe in the now decaying steamboat house we follow the tribal history from the beginning of Doom's dynasty. The New Orleans adven-ture skipped over in the other tales is sketched in here— the Parisian nobleman who helps Doom pass as a chief in that wide-open scene, the West Indian woman whom he gets pregnant and brings home to the plantation when he is chief in fact, and is married to "by a combination itinerant minister and slave trader" a month before Isse-tibbeha's birth. Marriage and slaveholding are interde-pendent in Faulkner's Old South. "After that Doom be-gan to acquire more slaves and to cultivate some of his own land, as the white people did."

14. The editor was Robert Linscott of Random House, as quoted by William Styron, "A Second Flowering," 10. Styron supports Cowley's em-phasis on the effect of Hemingway's work on Faulkner.

This phase of Indian slavery is seen in darker colors than in "A Justice." The blacks do not have much work, and can sustain their African ways, but they are first kept in pens like animals, and sometimes chased for sport with dogs. Faulkner can seem evasive where white guilt is in question, as when circling around Sutpen's refusal to acknowledge his black son in *Absalom, Absalom!* He shows what dehumanizing a race means when the Indians enter the slave trade in Issetibbeha's time. "Gathered in squatting conclave over the Negro question, squatting profoundly beneath the golden names over the doors of the steamboat," the elders debate what to do with their multiplying herd of blacks. Cannibalism is not feasible, for "that much flesh diet is not good for man." The alternative is to follow the white man's lead:

" 'Raise more Negroes by clearing more land to make corn to feed them, then sell them. We will clear the land and plant it with food and raise Negroes and sell them to the white man for money.'

'But what will we do with this money?' a third said.

'We will see,' the first said."

Thus capitalism is also satirized as the Indians succumb to it. Myrdal notes that some tribes "were active in the internal Negro slave trade." [15] A traveler in Indian Territory wrote of a visit to one Benjamin Franklin Colbert, a Chickasaw mixed blood of the family Faulkner mentions in "A Courtship," who owned twenty-five slaves. "He considers them about the best stock there is, as his increase is about four per year." [16]

The first proceeds of the trade finance Issetibbeha's Parisian trip, during which he is introduced into court circles, and acquires the gilt bed, "a pair of girandoles by

15. Gunnar Myrdal, *An American Dilemma* (New York, 1962), 124.
16. Gibson, *The Chickasaws*, 195.

whose light it was said that Pompadour arranged her hair while Louis smirked at his mirrored face across her powdered shoulder," and the fatal red slippers. The moral is Jeffersonian, tying old world corruption to slavery and the dynastic failure that, as always in Faulkner's work, slavery engenders. He does not exaggerate the Chickasaw attachment to European finery. At the end of the eighteenth century one chief, Wolf's Friend, "attended councils and other state functions in garments of "scarlet and silver lace, and in the heat of the day with a large crimson umbrella over him.' " [17] Issetibbeha grasps the absurdity of these trappings, with his own vein of frontier humor. Unable to sleep in the bed, he "quietly laughs and laughs" as his newest wife sneaks out to sleep on her pallet on the floor and return at daybreak. The joke is on the Indians, caught between the wilderness and white culture, and on life itself.

The affair of Issetibbeha, Moketubbe, and the slippers is a comic nightmare of degeneration. Like Sam Fathers, Faulkner's noblest savage, Moketubbe is the son of a black woman, whom his father noticed "when she was working in her shift in a melon patch." His name recalls the honored one of Moshuletubbe, a tough and wily Choctaw chief at the dispossession, but Moketubbe is a genetic disaster, with his broad, flat, Mongolian face and dropsical hands and feet, diseased with flesh from his childhood and alive only to the slippers. He cannot get his feet into them at three, is still publicly trying to do so at sixteen, and stealing the shoes to try to get them on at twenty-five. Issetibbeha unsuccessfully tries to give them to him, remembering how Doom's uncle met his

17. *Ibid.*, 80.

end. "I too like being alive, it seems," the fatalistic Indian says, an anticipation of the theme of the slave's flight. "And then Issetibbeha became dead, who was not old, and the shoes are Moketubbe's, since he is the Man now," Louis Berry sums it up. "What do you think of that?"

Moketubbe is summoned to the hunt in a scene as macabre as anything in Poe. On the steamboat deck an old man, barefoot, in a long linen frock coat and beaver hat (Kazin notes Faulkner's marvelous sense of costume in "Red Leaves") complains that the world has been going to the dogs ever since "the white men foisted their Negroes upon us." We leave him mumbling that the hunt for Doom's slave took not three days but three weeks, and enter the royal home:

> What had been the saloon of the steamboat was now a shell, rotting slowly; the polished mahogany, the carving glinting momentarily and fading through the mold in figures cabalistic and profound; the gutted windows were like cataracted eyes. It contained a few sacks of seed or grain, and the fore part of the running gear of a barouche, to the axle of which two C-springs rusted in graceful curves, supporting nothing. In one corner a fox cub ran steadily and soundlessly up and down a willow cage; three scrawny gamecocks moved in the dust, and the place was pocked and marked with their dried droppings.

One thinks of Doom on the foredeck as the steamboat is dragged through the wilderness. *Sic transit gloria mundi.* In a chair in the next room sits the new chief, "his round, smooth copper balloon of belly swelling above the bottom piece of a suit of linen underwear." Five feet tall and weighing 250 pounds, his eyes closed, "his flipper-like arms extended," he has worn the slippers since daylight, and shows no sign of life. "Upon his supine monstrous shape there was a colossal inertia, something profoundly immobile, beyond and impervious to flesh."

Life is motion, Faulkner liked to say. An incarnation of the opposite, even of death itself. Moketubbe is ludicrous, pathetic, with an aura about him of primordial evil. He apparently owes something to the huge chief Doramin in *Lord Jim*, who, however, is neither evil nor absurd—one sees how Faulkner's sensibility absorbs his reading. Moketubbe is compared to an effigy, a Malay god. Of Doramin, Conrad writes, "his bulk for a Malay was immense, but he did not look merely fat; he looked imposing, monumental. This motionless body, clad in rich stuffs, coloured silks, gold embroideries; this huge head, enfolded in a red-and-gold handkerchief; the flat, big, round face, wrinkled, furrowed. . . ." Conrad gives us a man with "something magnanimous and ruthless in his immobility," but allows for the comic aspect of the figure. "Doramin, waiting immovably in his big chair on the hillside, with the smoke of the guns spreading slowly over his big head, received the news with a deep grunt. When informed that his son was safe and leading the pursuit, he, without another sound, made a mighty effort to rise; his attendants hurried to his help, and, held up reverently, he shuffled with great dignity into a bit of shade where he laid himself down to sleep, covered entirely with a piece of white sheeting." [18] Faulkner takes this out of the heroic context and into that of mock epic, to set off the heroic endurance of the black fugitive.

The chief is also played off against the elders. For them the Man bears the life of the tribe, and what the slippers

18. Joseph Conrad, *Lord Jim* (New York, 1968), 158–66 and *passim*. Peter Irvine pointed out to me the resemblance of the two characters.

are to Moketubbe his inert flesh is to Three Basket, who tries to spark it into life, a life impossible in shoes that make him faint. In a travesty of all invocation of paternal example Basket lectures the apparently unconscious parricide on his duty to his father, who fetched the slave when Doom died. When the slippers are removed and Moketubbe finally responds, "his bare chest moving deep, as though he were rising from beyond his unfathomed flesh back into life, like up from the water, the sea," it is with the dark fatality of Moby Dick.

The deepening immobility of the Indian scenes prepares for the extraordinary intensity of the chase and capture. "Catch him and tell him that," says the boy fanning the chief to a remark that the slave might as well accept his fate. From the Indians in the steamboat the focus shifts to the black hidden in the barn, who knows that Issetibbeha's death means his own. "A Guinea man" who had been sold at fourteen to a trader off Cameroon— his origins are thus somewhat vague—"he had been Issetibbeha's body servant for twenty-three years." As he listens to the drums of his people in the swamp he gathers himself for every man's losing race: "He imagined himself springing out of the bushes, leaping among the drums on his bare, lean, greasy, invisible limbs. But he could not do that, because man leaped past life, into where death was; he dashed into death and did not die, because when death took a man, it took him just this side of the end of living. It was when death overran him from behind, still in life. The thin whisper of rat feet died in fainting gusts along the rafters." The slave's fate scarcely lifts the curse from his masters, as that of Frazer's dying god, or Oedipus, or Hamlet, redeems the tribe; but his six-day flight reestablishes the dignity of man.

Faulkner's image of black suffering is without parallel in nineteenth- or twentieth-century writing. The accounts of former slaves pale before the fugitive's agony—"panting, his nostrils flaring and pulsing, the hushed glare of his ceaseless eyeballs in his mud-daubed face as though they were worked from lungs." Like Christmas in *Light in August* he runs in a circle, with no place to go in the isolated Indian world. But where Christmas is also the victim of himself, his culture, and the arbitrary "Player" who works through Percy Grimm, the slave runs against death alone—the Indians merely wait him out. He attains universality in his brief hour on the stage. The acceptance of his fate, which may make him an unsatisfactory hero for black polemicists, lifts his story from melodrama to tragedy.

III

The concluding action falls into three parts—the assertion of the will to live, the capture, and death's summons; the point of view moves from that of the fugitive, to that of his pursuers, to the objective. After a day watching the guests arrive for the funeral he leaves the plantation via the creek bed, his ears filled with the howling of the dog which is tied to a tree beside the chief's horse. By sunset of the second day he has run thirty miles. Faulkner evokes a suspension of time and space like that which marathon runner Frank Shorter says keeps him from remembering what he thinks about when he runs: "A kind of numbness comes over him that feels at times like a trance, at times like a kind of meditation. In either case, time is compressed, the run seems much shorter than it is. And in marathons especially, the tendency is that the worst things are forgotten. The last six miles, by far the most difficult, are almost impossible to remember once the race is over." [19] Calvin Brown similarly recalls "an almost effortless running with no remembered beginning or forseeable end." He remembers and applies to "Red Leaves" the strategies of hare and hounds, including "doubling back and lying in hiding to rest a bit and gauge the lead when the pursuers passed" and climbing a tree to size up the pursuit, as does the slave.[20] All Faulkner's manhunts have these aspects of a game, in which the inevitability of capture strengthens the tension.

Contrasts with those not doomed to die give form to the chase and raise the emotional pitch. The slave is cut off from his own people now, "as though [by] an actual boundary between two different worlds"; when at night he follows the sound of drums into the creek bottoms, he is given meat and sent on his way. The harmlessness of his first pursuers—two paunchy middle-aged men in shirts and straw hats, their neatly rolled trousers under their arms—makes their fatality more terrible. Naked and covered with mud in the swamp, he wakes to hear them a few feet away, grumbling at the hard work of the chase. "One of them removed from his shirt tail a clot of cockleburs. 'Damn that Negro,' he said." To which his companion replies, "When have they ever been anything but a trial and a care to us?" It is a grim vision of paternalism when slavehunters sound like housewives sighing over their domestic servants or employers over labor.

The gulf between the powerless and the all-powerful is played off against the slave's vitality and the masters'

19. Shorter as quoted by Lawrence Shainberg, "The Obsessiveness of the Long-Distance Runner," *New York Times Magazine*, February 25, 1973, p. 33.
20. Calvin S. Brown, "Faulkner's Manhunts: Fact into Fiction," *Georgia Review*, XX (Winter, 1966), 389, 391.

lack of it. Looking down from a treetop into the plantation, he sees his "irrevocable doom" as Moketubbe joins the pursuit in his litter. He meets an Indian on a footlog in the swamp—"the Negro gaunt, lean, hard, tireless and desperate," the Indian again the embodiment of inertia. The Darwinian theme is implicit in these polarities. It is the blacks who will survive. But the individual will not, although he eats a line of ants moving up a log to meet their doom in him. The jocular comparisons of slave to dinner guest and ants to "salted nuts from a dish" provide in their absurd disparateness another protest against the nature of things.

When the cottonmouth moccasin strikes him as he is stalking a frog in the swamp, he accepts his death and discovers the depth and extent of his desire to live: " 'Olé, Grandfather,' the Negro said. He touched its head and watched it slash him again across his arm, and again, with thick, raking, awkward blows, 'It's that I do not wish to die,' he said. Then he said it again." At Virginia, Faulkner commented: "The snake episode was to show that man when he knows he's going to die thinks that he can accept death, but he doesn't—he doesn't, really. The Negro at the time, he said, I'm already dead, it doesn't matter, the snake can bite me because I'm already dead, but yet at the end he still wanted to put off—that man will cling to life, that in preference—between grief and nothing, man will take grief always." [21] The "Olé, Grandfather" has a literal force it lacks in "The Old People" and "The Bear," for the cottonmouth is the man's totem ancestor, and actually prepares him for death, beginning

21. Gwynn and Blotner (eds.), *Faulkner in the University*, 25. Here he echoes Harry in *The Wild Palms*. "Between grief and nothing I will take grief," Harry says when choosing to live with his memories rather than kill himself.

the separation of his body from his will. The sacramental vital force of snakes is symbolized by their peculiar proximity to the earth, their perfection of the circle (when seen with head in mouth) and powers of self-renewal. African snake cults were brought to Mississippi from Louisiana, like Doom's slaves, and the "Great Moccasin" was addressed in voodoo ceremonies in New Orleans in Faulkner's time.[22] He combines this with the patriarchal Indian totemism, which the slave would have absorbed after serving Issetibbeha so long. On the way to death the black tells Basket of greeting the snake as it struck him. He maintains a relationship to nature and to fate now apparently lost to the Indians themselves.

From this episode we return to the pursuers, to the comic perspective which breaks the tension and enables the writer to build it up again. "Moketubbe took the slippers with him." The no-longer-pristine trophies of another world are seen "lying upon the supine, obese shape just barely alive, carried through swamp and brier by swinging relays of men who bore steadily all day long the crime and its object, on the business of the slain." The scene evokes a rare echo of Dante in Faulkner: "To Moketubbe it must have been as though, himself immortal, he were being carried rapidly through hell by doomed spirits which, alive, had contemplated his disaster, and, dead, were oblivious partners to his damnation." From time to time the bearers stop so he can wear the slippers for a while, and they must stop again when "honor has been served"—in the excitement of nearing

22. See "Anatol Pierre" in "Black Magic and Chance," Langston Hughes and Arna Bontemps (eds.), *The Book of Negro Folklore* (New York, 1958), 188. Pierre the teacher—who is an octoroon—tells the initiate to "call on Great Moccasin for all kinds of power and also to have him stir up the particular spirit I may need for a specific task."

the quarry they forget, and the chief faints. The southern writer parodies the burden of a noble tradition while he underscores the suffering and courage of the slave.

The black has the will to endure, to savor the essence of life to the end, running on a motionless and frozen landscape in a Faulknerian suspension of time. Three days from the snakebite he is finally cornered in the swamp; and by then he has thrown off the effects, a mark of his toughness, although his arm first swelled and then shriveled to the size of a child's. He shows the scouts the arm—they do not want him too badly hurt to be of service in the other world—and asks for a hatchet to chop it off, asks them for a quick death then and there. But "Tomorrow is today also" for the Chickasaws, whose philosophical patience serves to retard the clock. Faulkner simultaneously elevates the scene, showing the evening star and the constellations above the squatting men covered with gnats and mosquitoes and the swamp from which they are waked by a voice shouting and talking in the middle of the night. They are the chorus, the black is the hero, drama returns to its roots in human sacrifice.

In the capture scene, Faulkner uses a tragic mask and attains a formal catharsis:

> Dawn came; a white crane flapped slowly across the jonquil sky. Basket was awake. "Let us go now," he said. "It is today."
>
> Two Indians entered the swamp, their movements noisy. Before they reached the Negro they stopped, because he began to sing. They could see him, naked and mud-caked, sitting on a log, singing. They squatted silently a short distance away, until he finished. He was chanting something in his own language, his face lifted to the rising sun. His voice was clear, full, with a quality wild and sad. "Let him

have time," the Indians said, squatting, patient, waiting.
He ceased and they approached. He looked back and up
at them through the cracked mud mask. His eyes were
bloodshot, his lips cracked upon his square short teeth.
The mask of mud appeared to be loose on his face, as if he
might have lost flesh since he put it there; he held his left
arm close to his breast. From the elbow down it was caked
and shapeless with black mud. They could smell him, a
rank smell. He watched them quietly until one touched
him on the arm. "Come," the Indian said. "You ran well.
Do not be ashamed."

The greatness of this passage survives any possible analy-
sis of its union of intelligence with feeling, form with the
life which sustains it. It is of a piece with Yeats's "tragic
joy." The Indian's compliment is not undercut by the
fact that the pursuers have not run at all, have held to a
slow pace with much complaint. The irony is strong, yet
the masters are not subject to the same conditions as the
slave and can make overdue acknowledgment of his manhood, vicariously participating in the antique virtue
which he represents. Do not be ashamed to be caught,
then, for this is the race no one wins—"when death took
a man, it took him just this side of the end of living."
Faulkner has redeemed the commonplace. Such are the
aesthetic possibilities of slavery, for a writer with the
classical-Christian sense of death as the final master.

This mastership is the substance of the last scene, in the
latter part of which the word *come* is sounded six times.
Three Basket is the speaker, the black is set off against
the Indian community, his agony against the inevitable
and implacable force that condemns him. Issetibbeha's
body and his horse and dog wait beside the grave when
he is brought in, looming above his captors. "The already

moving guests halted, pausing, looking back, some with pieces of meat in their hands, as the Negro looked about at their faces with his wild, restrained, unceasing eyes." Man's inhumanity to man, the barrier between the living and the about-to-die, the fact that "man will cling to life," all are present here. The Indians offer him food that he does not want and water he cannot swallow and will not stop trying to drink, while Basket summons him in measured repetitions that leave no way out. The shadows of noon on the slope where the well is, part way down toward the quarters, sharpen the sweetness and the terror of man's fate, and this is fused with the historical experience of the blacks in the final tableau:

> "Come," Basket said.
> "Wait," the Negro said. He dipped the gourd again and tilted it against his face, beneath his ceaseless eyes. Again they watched his throat working and the unswallowed water sheathing broken and myriad down his chin, channeling his caked chest. They waited, patient, grave, decorous, implacable; clansman and guest and kin. Then the water ceased, though still the empty gourd tilted higher and higher, and still his black throat aped the vain motion of his frustrated swallowing. A piece of water-loosened mud carried away from his chest and broke at his muddy feet, and in the empty gourd they could hear his breath: ah-ah-ah.
> "Come," Basket said, taking the gourd from the Negro and hanging it back in the well.

The Indian's tact and the naturalistic images, the water washing through the mud and carrying a piece away, enforce the classical idea of mortality. This seems far from the horror of men preying on their fellow man, on a racial scapegoat, but Faulkner makes the combination work, integrating different realms of his experience. The Christian background of the South contributes to the vision of black suffering here.

The will to live in "Red Leaves" is Faulkner's own. "It's that I do not wish to die," the black repeats when struck by the snake, and the words reverberate through the last scene. Thirty years after writing the story, during his last days, Faulkner echoed his protagonist when speaking to his friend and doctor, Felix Linder of Oxford: "He walked a half mile . . . a good half mile down here two or three times and told me he didn't want to die. I'd be sitting on the porch there. 'Felix . . .' he'd say. He called me Felix. 'I don't want to die.' That's what he told me." Dr. Linder explains that Faulkner was often in great pain from the accidents he had riding his jumping horses, pain which could make him cry, but refused pain-killing drugs. Like the black in this story, "he was tough as you ever saw." "I says, 'I could give you something to keep you from suffering. I could do that. I'll be glad to.' William says, 'That ain't what I want.' " [23] The doctor adds that it was hard to tell what he wanted, but Faulkner's comment on "Red Leaves" makes this clear enough. "Between grief and nothing, man will take grief always."

On this level of his being Faulkner does justice to black experience as few others have, as he himself could only do with the Indians as surrogate masters. The story shows how the principle which allows men to work other men in the fields allows them to kill a man, because he is only a piece of property. One could conceivably argue

23. Felix Linder, "A Gentleman of the First Order," in James W. Webb and A. Wigfall Green (eds.), *William Faulkner of Oxford* (Baton Rouge, 1965), 173.

that the slave, in accepting the system by which he suffers so, in submitting to his death, is a white man's black hero, but this is to subject art to the politics of image-making, and the bias is bad history. Eugene Genovese has commented on the falsity of searching for militant opposition in the record of slavery and dismissing other attitudes as collaborationist, the result of, for one thing, brain-washing: "If a slave helped to keep himself psychologically intact by breaking his master's hoe, he might also have achieved the same result by a special effort to come to terms with his God, or by loving a woman who shared his burdens, or even by aspiring to be the best worker on the plantation. . . . For the most part the best that the slaves could do was to live, not merely physically, but with as much inner autonomy as was humanly possible." [24] From this point of view Faulkner's slave is heroic indeed. Not a rounded character like Dilsey and Lucas Beauchamp, who emerge from the plantation background, he sustains his identity on the wilderness stage; he lives.

The characterization of the Indians, out of place now in the wilderness, caught between their old traditions and a commercial-agricultural society, is less sympathetic than in the other three stories. They take their place in the well-known American class hierarchy within which one minority victimizes another. Had the Choctaws, Chickasaws, and Cherokees not been deprived of their lands they might have developed into a race between white and black men in the South, like the "assimilados" of the Portuguese African colonies. "Red Leaves" does not make this an attractive possibility. The ritual killing

24. Eugene D. Genovese, "American Slaves and Their History," *New York Review of Books*, XV (December 3, 1970), 35, 43.

is Faulkner's *donné*. Paradoxically, in the last scene it partly restores the dignity of the tribe, and the elders' awareness of the black's humanity humanizes them. With Moketubbe offstage, their pride and decorum stand out as distinctly Indian—a legacy to Sam Fathers.

This is Faulkner's last vision of the Indian within a basically Indian society. In *Go Down, Moses* Sam Fathers is a link with that society, a symbol of the past within the new white world, through which one can romanticize the ancient life of the Chickasaws, the life they lost on contact with the whites. "Red Leaves" is apparently far away, yet strong continuities exist. Faulkner's noble savage is part black and a former slave, while Doom's background role shows how the Indians prefigured the plantation South. The alternative to the plantation remains the ritual of the hunt, no manhunt now, yet one involving the death of Sam Fathers as well as of Old Ben and Lion. The dramatic economy of "Red Leaves" yields to rhetorical expansion and celebration through the white youth's consciousness. Again, however, affirmation of life against death is the motive of Faulkner's art; and Sam Fathers and Isaac McCaslin, caretakers of the wilderness and the Indian tradition, are the spiritual descendants of Issetibbeha's nameless slave.

VII ✌ Sam Fathers and *Go Down, Moses*

In *Go Down, Moses* the uniquely Faulknerian world of the Indian stories, with their roots in history, their humor, and their imaginative freedom, gives way to an Indian legend out of mythology and American romance. Faulkner goes back to Cooper and Melville for the themes of manhood in nature under the tutelage of the darkskinned savage, of the great hunt in the dying wilderness. He transforms the Sam Fathers of "A Justice" into the master of the hunting ritual and fuses the hunting experience of his own community with totemism and animistic beliefs. "The Old People" establishes the ritual within the frontier-plantation South, and in "The Bear" Faulkner detaches it from the social structure, as manhood in the hunt becomes the basis for Isaac's rejection of title to the land. His central theme, readers and critics of "The Bear" would probably agree, is the discovery of morality in an elemental nature man seems doomed to destroy.

We are far here from his introduction to hunting as a boy, prepared for by walks with Mammy Callie and presided over by his own father. It is "a case of the sorry, shabby world that don't quite please you, so you create one of your own," as he rather grandly says.[1] The limitations of reality in this case involved the painful accident which had deferred his initiation to the big woods till adulthood. When rabbit hunting, John Faulkner writes, William had killed one of the two beagle hounds his father bought the boys. "He dropped his gun and brought the dog home in his arms. When he got there he laid the little dog on the porch and went to his room and locked himself in and cried. He was about fourteen, I think, and did not take up another gun until he was grown and went on the deer hunt below Batesville." [2] Something of this survives when Boon brings Lion back to camp to die, and in the elegiac ground tone of "The Bear." "There was a man and a dog too this time." In the article, "Mississippi," Faulkner speaks of having "shared in the yearly ritual of 'Old Ben,' " who was killed with a knife by "the youth [himself]'s father's foreman . . . to save a hound which he, Boon Hogganbeck, loved." [3] His insistence on his imagined world is associated with the old wound.

His hunting experience in the 1930s was the immediate source of his image of an epic boyhood. Faulkner began hunting seriously after he settled down at Rowan Oak, and in the people and the discipline he found a new enthusiasm for his land. While Sam Fathers and Boon were drawn from presences of his childhood, friends like Uncle Ike Roberts and Uncle Bud Miller also served as

1. Frederick Gwynn and Joseph L. Blotner (eds.), *Faulkner in the University: Class Conferences in the University of Virginia, 1957–58* (Charlottesville, Va., 1959), 59.

2. John Faulkner, *My Brother Bill: An Affectionate Reminiscence* (New York, 1963), 90.

3. "Mississippi," in James B. Meriwether (ed.), *Essays, Speeches, and Public Letters by William Faulkner* (New York, 1965), 37.

models, and the storytelling that was among the pleasures of the hunt stimulated his tales. Although solemnized in "The Bear," this was to John Cullen simply "the lying contest." Another of Faulkner's hunting companions says, "I don't know whether he ever killed a bear or not, but he'd make you think he had," and Cullen believed he had killed his first deer at fifteen or sixteen.[4] His greatest tall tale turns the storytelling blacksmith into Ike's instructor-priest. The writer thereby gains perspective on the rest of his material.

Sam Fathers' role is the only facet of these stories, apparently, without a local source. There were no self-proclaimed Indians on Faulkner's hunts, or blacks in roles other than those of Ash and Tennie's Jim. In the Old South, Indians and blacks had sometimes been involved as guides but were not spokesmen for the wilderness. Sam's literary ancestry is plain. "The wild man not even one generation from the woods, childless, kinless, peopleless," he derives from Cooper's Indians, from Chingachgook and his son Uncas, the last of the Mohicans; and, with Isaac McCaslin, from Natty Bumppo. His relationship with the young Ike also recalls those of Queequeg and Ishmael, Jim and Huck. In these nineteenth-century novels the conflict of nature and society acquires its distinctively American cast. Man meets man on terms of equality, apart from socially contrived fears.

Neither Queequeg nor Jim, however, is a father figure.

4. The quotations are from John B. Cullen and Floyd Watkins, *Old Times in the Faulkner Country* (Chapel Hill, N.C., 1961), 38, and Claude Maxwell Smith, "He Just Wanted to Be Old Bill," in James W. Webb and A. Wigfall Green (eds.), *William Faulkner of Oxford* (Baton Rouge, 1965), 66. See also Cullen and Watkins, *Old Times*, 13.

The influence of *Moby-Dick* upon "The Bear" looms large, but Melville's interest is in brotherhood. Huck's relationship with Jim is based on mutual protection, and the loyalty for which he consigns himself to hell is not comparable to Ike's profound deference to the Indian-Negro. Faulkner's predecessors lack the patriarchal southern tradition, and their nineteenth-century assumptions about progress and civilization limit their piety toward the past of man. Faulkner denounces the rape of the wilderness as Cooper does but without the latter's ambivalence about the end results. And where Melville makes Queequeg's religion as good as ours, Sam Fathers is our spiritual guide. He retires when no longer needed, as spiritual fathers do, from tribal puberty rites to the *Divine Comedy*. He represents the wisdom of the peoples Faulkner's own race has suppressed. Literature compensates for history.

Sam Fathers emerges as the novel does from the magazine stories behind it. He does not exist in "Lion" (1935), which recounts the deaths of Lion and Old Ben, the visit to the graves, and the discovery of Boon at the Gum Tree. The boy is named Quentin and Uncle Ike McCaslin is the master of the hunt. In the *Harper's* "Old People" (1940) and the *Saturday Evening Post* "Bear" (1942) Sam Fathers presides, marking the unnamed narrator's face with the blood of his first kill and showing him the great antlered deer, preparing him for the encounter with Old Ben. Here, however, he must compete with an orthodox southern father, introduced in "Lion," who takes part in the hunt and has the speeches interpreting the vision of the deer and the boy's inability to shoot Old Ben which are given to McCaslin Edmonds in *Go Down,*

Moses. The father's removal in the final versions of the tales, where the initiate becomes Isaac McCaslin, brings the ritual into focus.

"THE OLD PEOPLE"

"The Old People" is a curiously neglected story. It has a purity of form and tone which "The Bear," with all its grandeur, lacks. The initiation scenes at beginning and end frame the portrait of the "old dark man" in whom the wilderness heritage defines itself against that of slavery. Ikkemotubbe's son now, Sam Fathers is cut off from his heroic past like others in Faulkner's world, but recreates this with and through the boy. In the process it is universalized. Faulkner's title refers both to the Indians and to the larger wisdom of the past, before men lost the right relationship to the land. The trembling boy's achievement of manhood becomes a poem of natural piety.

The picture of Sam Fathers overlaps with "A Justice." Again he is remembered sitting in the door of the blacksmith shop, or working there, at his own pace rather than at the white man's bidding. But this is "when he was not in the woods," "when the woods had not drawn him." His place in the November deer and bear hunt shapes the boy's identification with him and ambition to be a hunter and a man. Sam is standing behind Ike when, at age eight, so the tall tale runs, "he shot his first running rabbit with his first gun and almost with the first load it ever carried." Two years later Sam can say, in the tones of Daniel Boone or Leatherstocking, "I done taught you all there is of this settled country." While waiting on the fox or coon or wild turkey, Sam talks of the old days and the People whom he cannot himself remember, until it seems to the boy that time has been reversed, and the white and black men have not yet come into the land.

Again Faulkner is "sublimating the actual into apocryphal." John Faulkner associates their childhood visits to the farm with the fall, "the time of year to talk about hunting, too early to go yet but time to begin thinking about it," and he assumed the "Negro blacksmith" was telling Bill hunting stories. Faulkner gives his friend the freedom of the wilderness and the authority of a guide, setting the tale a generation closer to the frontier to make this feasible. Sam Fathers no longer has to establish an Indian identity. In the romantic tradition he becomes the chief's son, is so known by both the blacks and McCaslin Edmonds, who in "The Bear" argues that Ike also owns the land through Sam. Although Sam is socially a black, the boy senses a deference to him in Boon Hogganbeck, whose strain of Indian blood is not royal.

From one point of view the black is being built up as an Indian, a southerner's compromise with the color line. In the early tale, Sam "says his words" as blacks do and has Negro hair. He becomes a man "with hair like a horse's mane which even at seventy showed no trace of white and a face which showed no age until he smiled, whose only visible trace of Negro blood was a slight dullness of the hair and the fingernails, and something else which you did notice about the eyes." The "something else" is defined by McCaslin as the expression of a wild man who has been caged, "the knowledge that for a while that part of his blood had been the blood of slaves." Faulkner makes it a small part by making Sam Fathers' mother a quadroon, "who had bequeathed him not only the blood of slaves but even a little of the very blood which had enslaved it; himself his own battleground, the scene of his own vanquishment and mausoleum of his own defeat." The character thus represents the Old South as well as the old people.

In becoming Doom's son, Sam acquires a father who will not acknowledge him, as Old Carothers and Sutpen will not acknowledge their black sons. In "A Justice," he is the product of a simple case of adultery—"a fine yellow man," the chief says—but in "The Old People," Doom marries off his pregnant mistress to one of his slaves. The name Fathers acquires a new ironical dimension. The burden of slavery and racism is underscored. Faulkner is supported by the Chickasaw and Choctaw legislation on marriage with blacks, which a chief would have had to sustain. That the Five Civilized Tribes repudiated their former slaves in the division of their lands in Indian Territory also stands behind the characterization.

The other side of the Indian rejection of the taint of slavery is the black's identification with a purported Indian ancestor. To Faulkner himself Sam Fathers is "the old dark man sired on both sides by savage kings." Just so he affirms the African origins of Lucas Beauchamp, "most of whose blood," Roth Edmonds reflects, "was pure ten thousand years when my own anonymous beginnings became mixed enough to produce me." The tradition of the noble savage in English literature had included blacks, and Faulkner follows this.[5] But Lucas and Sam, in a novel of the Deep South published in 1942, cannot see their fathers as African kings. As the one identifies with his white grandfather, Old Carothers, the

5. H. N. Fairchild discusses this in *The Noble Savage: A Study in Romantic Naturalism* (New York, 1928), 403–406, 466–67, 474–75, and *passim*.

other does so with the Chickasaw chief and the wilderness itself.

Sam Fathers is a former slave for the sake of the novel as a whole, an Indian for the hunt, the wilderness, the frontier past, and the profound effect that, through the romantic movement, these had on the American imagination. "Let me go," he says, sounding the author's larger theme, and his Indian blood gives him a destination, an alternative to the plantation. It is a functional equivalent for later doctrines of black culture and black pride, but not, of course, exclusivist. In the background the white boy thinks, "Just three years more and Cass says I can go." The wilderness is freedom for his people too.

The theme of the hunt as meeting ground of race and caste has its regional roots. Hunting was a common culture in the South. "The small farmer, the frontiersman, the poor white—and frequently the Negro—all were hunters," Clarence Gohdes explains in presenting a volume of selected accounts of this sport among the gentry. Men hunted to improve the evening meal as well as for pleasure, as is still sometimes true in the country. Even under slavery, Gohdes suggests, roles were modified in the process. "A farmer possessed of one or two slaves was as likely to take to the field in their company as he was to join his neighbors in pursuit of game." Blacks generally had subordinate places in the hunts of planters and their guests, but there were exceptions: "In many localities certain Negroes or Indians were numbered among the expert Nimrods of the community, and their society was at times apparently courted." [6]

6. Clarence Gohdes, *Hunting in the Old South* (Baton Rouge, 1967), xiii, xvi.

The Old South is also a source of the boy's baptism in the deer's blood, generally thought to reflect the ritual of primitive tribes. One of the episodes in Gohdes' book—in which a black participates—includes such an initiation:

> We all rode to the spot [where the animal fell], to congratulate our novice on his first exploit in sylvan warfare—when, as he stopped to examine the direction of his shot, our friend Loveleap slipped his knife into the throat of the deer, and before his purpose could be guessed at, bathed his face with the blood of his victim. (This, you must know, *is hunter's law* with us, on the killing of a first deer). As our young sportsman started up from the ablution—his face flaring like an Indian chief's in all the splendor of war paint—Robin the hunter touched his cap and thus accosted him:
>
> "Maussa Tickle, if you wash off dat blood dis day—you neber hab luck again so long as you hunt."
>
> "Wash it off!" cried we all, with one accord; "who ever heard of such a folly. He can be no true sportsman, who is ashamed of such a livery." [7]

The author is William Elliott, a Harvard-educated planter whose *Carolina Sports by Land and Water* appeared in 1846 and was several times reprinted. Faulkner could have seen it anywhere and, steeped in Frazer, he would have been pleased to find this "hunter's law" documented. His debt to Elliott may not end here, for the planter also tells of killing a wounded buck with a knife, after a chase resembling that of Old Ben. It is the veteran white hunter who marks the novice in *Carolina Sports*;

7. William Elliott, "A Day at Chee-Ha," *Carolina Sports by Land and Water* (Columbia, S.C., 1918), 155. See also Gohdes, *Hunting in the Old South*, 6–7.

but the look of an Indian chief and the black hunter
Robin's affirmation of the ceremony could have suggested
shifting this to Sam. The initiate, a newly married man,
becomes the twelve-year-old Ike; the jovial sportsman's
tones give way to the seriousness with which a boy would
take the experience.

Through Ike and Sam, Faulkner gives it transcendent
meaning. The opening lines of the story go back to Gene-
sis, to the void and the original "Let there be light":

> At first there was nothing. There was the faint, cold, steady
> rain, the gray and constant light of the late November
> dawn, with the voices of the hounds converging somewhere
> in it, and toward them. Then Sam Fathers . . . touched his
> shoulder and he began to shake, not with any cold. Then
> the buck was there. He did not come into sight; he was just
> there, looking not like a ghost but as if all of light were
> condensed in him and he the source of it, not only moving
> in it but disseminating it, already running, seen first as you
> always see the deer, in that split second after he has already
> seen you, already slanting away in that first soaring bound,
> the antlers even in that dim light looking like a small rock-
> ing chair on his head.

"Whence does he spring, the deer, the deer, the deer,"
goes a song of the Chippewas.[8] Again, for Faulkner, life
is motion. The running deer disseminating light is a creation image on the writer's Sistine ceiling. The last precise, humorous touch sustains the realism of the hunt,
but the animal's miraculous advent and the word *ghost*
prepare for the great buck Sam Fathers shows the boy
later the same day, "coming down the ridge as if it were
walking out of the very sound of the horn which related

8. "Song," in John Bierhorst (ed.), *In the Trail of the Wind: American
Indian Poems and Ritual Orations* (New York, 1971), 53.

its death." "Since man is mortal," Faulkner said in his
Paris Review interview, "the only immortality possible
for him is to leave something behind him that is immortal since it will always move." [9]

The shot follows, and Sam marks Ike with the blood,
a pagan confirmation which, in its implications of sexual
manhood, may be contrasted with Joe Christmas' unsuccessful self-baptism in the blood of the sheep. The
boy is now the spiritual heir of the wilderness, and its
immortality is in turn shored up and extended by his act
and faith. He is simultaneously confirmed as the heir of
his own people. The pageantry of the hunt—Sam's ringing horn, the wave of dogs tasting the blood—brings on
"the men, the true hunters—Walter Ewell whose rifle
never missed, and Major de Spain and old General Compson, and the boy's cousin, McCaslin Edmonds," representatives of the traditions of Faulkner's land, to whom Sam
certifies that he "done all right." Ike's ties to Sam Fathers
and to his own forebears are in balance as they are not in
"The Bear." "The Old People" is written as though he
will inherit the land and leave his descendants in it as his
grandfather had done.

He is also bound to the deer he kills, the appointed
victim. Looking back, the old Ike of "Delta Autumn"
puts the obligation into words: "I slew you; my bearing
must not shame your quitting life. My conduct forever
onward must become your death." It is the aristocratic
code of the South of Walter Scott, and of General Lee.
McCaslin elaborates the code in "The Bear," defining
the "truths of the heart" as "courage and honor and pride

9. "Interview with Jean Stein vanden Heuvel," in James B. Meriwether and Michael Millgate (eds.), *Lion in the Garden: Interviews with
William Faulkner, 1926–1962* (New York, 1968), 253.

and pity and love of justice and of liberty." To the boy of "The Old People" the deer and he are bound past death; the chase is transcendent as on Keats's Grecian urn. The big woods through which the wagon jounces home that afternoon are "less than inimical now and never to be inimical again, since the buck still and forever leaped, the shaking gun-barrels coming constantly and forever steady at last, and out of his instant of immortality the buck sprang, forever immortal." Ike is ready for the communion which completes the experience of killing one's first deer. He can see the great buck whom Sam Fathers greets as a totem-avatar of his ancestors.

The characterization of the old man precedes and prepares for this, and Faulkner creates another character to represent the tradition passed on through Sam. The full-blooded Chickasaw Jobaker, a hermit whom only Sam can approach, is plausible for the 1870s—he dies when Ike is nine, which, according to "The Bear," would be 1876. He authenticates the greeting of "Oleh, Grandfather": "And, perhaps once a month the boy would find them in Sam's shop—the two old men squatting on their heels on the dirt floor, talking in a mixture of Negroid English and flat hill dialect and now and then a phrase of that old tongue which as time went on and the boy squatted there too listening, he began to learn." This scene does not appear in "A Justice," and it is plainly an improvement on Faulkner's boyhood. He heard no Indian conversation in the blacksmith shop in the 1900s. If he heard any purportedly Indian words, the one he remembered is Caribbean-African in its kinships. Jobaker is a link with the whole primeval world before the red men "owned" the land as the whites now "own" it. His spiritual authority is established with his mysterious funeral. His grave is never found; his hut is burned by Sam Fathers, who fires on some black intruders just as Boon threatens to fire on McCaslin Edmonds at Sam's grave. With Jobaker's death Sam withdraws to the forest, shedding his servile blood. His solitude is dissolved in the "profound, sentient, brooding" life of the big woods.

The vision of the deer, the forest patriarch, is one of the triumphs the Indian theme makes possible for Faulkner. It is grounded in the sometimes mysterious actualities of hunting, as elaborated in tall tales. The great antlered buck is stalked by the true hunters but escapes, walking within a few feet of the old man and the boy, while up the ridge a young deer is killed in what appear to be the old one's tracks. It is as though the one had been substituted that the other might live, and the majestic survivor, "tremendous unhurried, slanting and tilting its head to pass the antlers through the undergrowth," is an emblem of immortal life. Sam's greeting in the old tongue expresses a hunter's wonder and awe.

Faulkner makes this the boy's initiation to the forest and the old people. The line between outsider and initiate is clear. Boon, who cannot shoot at all but has Indian blood, sees the animal break cover, while Walter, the crack shot, does not see the deer and remains as skeptical as the British ship captain is of the existence of Moby Dick. The harsh jesting of the men intensifies Ike's excitement, which deepens as Sam leads them through the woods and the gray afternoon. When Sam sends the other two ahead the breathless expectation of the morning returns to him: "Then once more he and Sam stood motionless together against a tremendous pin oak in a little thicket, and again there was nothing. There was only the soaring and somber solitude in the dim light, there was the thin murmur of the faint cold rain which had not ceased all day." It is the church of the forest primeval. The wilderness' breathing becomes identified with Ike's heartbeat very much in the way that in *Heart of Darkness* Marlow confuses the beat of the drum in the forest where he will find Kurtz with the beating of his heart. Blood speaks to blood, the "precivilized" part of man's nature enters into his consciousness in the experience which, in these so different stories, is maturity:

> Then, as if it had waited for them to find their positions and become still, the wilderness breathed again. It seemed to lean inward above them, above himself and Sam and Walter and Boon in their separate lurking-places, tremendous, attentive, impartial and omniscient, the buck moving in it somewhere, not running yet since he had never been pursued, not frightened yet and never fearsome but just alert also as they were alert, perhaps already circling back, perhaps quite near, perhaps conscious also of the eye of the ancient immortal Umpire. Because he was just twelve then, and that morning something had happened to him: in less than a second he had ceased forever to be the child he was yesterday. Or perhaps that made no difference, perhaps even a city-bred man, let alone a child, could not have understood it; perhaps only a country-bred one could comprehend loving the life he spills. He began to shake again.

Glauco Cambon has shown how Faulkner's prose works here, how he animistically personifies the forest through the "fear and trembling" of the boy. The adjective *tremendous,* used for the deer as well as the big woods, "recovers its original numinous charge," becoming "awe-inspiring," "holy." [10] The word also shows Faulkner's base in the tall tale, and he sustains a hunter's realism. The boy awaits the sylvan god with a nervousness he knows will leave when it is time to raise the gun.

As Cambon says, we may see the buck coming down the ridge as an apparition induced by Sam's influence on Ike and the expectations of his *rite de passage*, by his increased awareness of and resistance to death itself. But "the apparition is treated as a natural phenomenon, and thus becomes more convincing." He has been made privy to the secret life of the forest by "something Sam had had in his turn of his vanished and forgotten people." For Sam and him they now return in the buck's form:

> It did not even alter its course, not fleeing, not even running, just moving with that winged and effortless ease with which deer move, passing within twenty feet of them, its head high and the eye not proud and not haughty but just full and wild and unafraid, and Sam standing beside the boy now, his right arm raised at full length, palm-outward, speaking in that tongue which the boy had learned from listening to him and Jobaker in the blacksmith shop, while up the ridge Walter Ewell's horn was still blowing them in to a dead buck.
>
> "Oleh, Chief," Sam said. "Grandfather."

In some respects this passage is African rather than Indian. The dead are not only part of the surrounding intangible life, but can and do take concrete form when the more effective presence is necessary. The materialization of spirit, the ubiquity of ancestors, and the imposition of lineage are found in various West African cultures.

10. Glauco Cambon, "Faulkner's 'The Old People': The Numen-Engendering Style," *Southern Review*, n. s., I (January, 1965), 104. The quotation in the next paragraph is from p. 102 of this essay.

The specificity of Faulkner's totemism, which is Indian, here establishes the hidden identity of the initiate with his god. Sam Fathers *is* Grandfather. One recalls that Ike's father's name is Buck, and one can make a case for the boy's identity with the young spiked-horn buck who is killed in the great one's place. The biblical parallel supports this reading of Ike's initiation, in a sense a sacrifice that the forest may live. Walter and Boon can grumble and speculate about the little buck in the big one's tracks, but there are more things in heaven and earth than are dreamt of in their philosophy.[11]

McCaslin Edmonds' commentary rounds out the story. The earth is charged with the presences of those before us, he says to the boy in their shared bed at Major de Spain's that night, with the "scoured and icy" stars outside. The organic cycle is the rule: "The earth dont want to just keep things, hoard them; it wants to use them again. Look at the seed, the acorns; at what happens even to carrion when you try to bury it: it refuses too, seethes and struggles too until it reaches light and air again, hunting the sun still." All the life of the past, then, "could not have been invented and created just to be thrown away." Faulkner rejects this tendency of American civilization:

11. In Yoruba and other West African mythologies the forest spirits have the habit of encountering human beings on the road, often in animal form. In the ChiWara legend of Sudanic West Africa the spirit of the antelope presides over agriculture and especially the planting of grain. Ancestors may be represented by a deer or an antelope mask in the dance, in the secret societies of West African forest cultures. An African reading this passage in Faulkner would probably say that a spirit has taken on the mask of the deer in order to communicate some message. I am indebted to Philip Allen, a writer and teacher on African and black American culture, for this understanding of West African religious symbolism.

Think of all that has happened here, on this earth. All the blood hot and strong for living, pleasuring, that has soaked back into it. For grieving and suffering too, of course, but still getting something out of it for all that, getting a lot out of it, because after all you don't have to continue to bear what you believe is suffering; you can always choose to stop that, put an end to that. And even suffering and grieving is better than nothing; there is only one thing worse than not being alive, and that's shame.

The rhetoric is familiar. "Between grief and nothing man will take grief, always," Faulkner says of the slave's experience in "Red Leaves." Ike will learn of grief and suffering, of the mortality of Indians and blacks and the forest in the modern world. But the nobility of the hunting ritual is redemptive. Lengthy, theatrical, fusing romantic eloquence with the vigor of the vernacular, the speech is Faulkner's response to the soliloquies of Hamlet and Macbeth, an affirmative answer, at this point in his life, to the eternally urgent questions they raise.[12]

McCaslin is Ike's foster father, and this scene balances those in the forest with Sam. It recalls "A Justice," where the boy, also twelve years old, moves from Sam Fathers' orbit to his grandfather's, and looks forward to the conversations in "The Bear." In "The Bear" he chooses his "spirit's father" over his social one. In "The Old People"

12. He worked it over carefully, and there are substantial improvements from the typescript at the University of Virginia. Instead of "all the blood hot and strong for living, pleasuring, that had soaked back into it," the typescript has "all the blood hot and strong for what it wanted, in conflict with other hot strong blood for what they each or both wanted." In the typescript, the boy says of the spirits of the departed, "They are dear to us," which becomes "There is plenty of room for us and them too"; and McCaslin's hand "grips" him instead of "touching his flank beneath the covers," as in the published version. Faulkner's revision both intensifies the poetry and keeps the speech from falling over into sentimentality.

wilderness and society are still in harmony, and the wisdom of the fathers descends naturally to the sons. McCaslin has the last words, confirming the validity of Ike's experience. "Steady," he says to the trembling boy. "Sam took me in there once after I killed my first deer."

"THE BEAR"

In "The Bear" the Indian background supports the legend of the big woods and the great hunters who are the last of their kind, the chivalry of a society cursed by slavery and the violation of the land. Faulkner treats the passing of the southern frontier as the loss of the new world Eden, and integrates Ike McCaslin's coming of age with the last great chase. With Francis Parkman, he could have said that he aimed "to portray the American forest and the American Indian at the moment when both received their final doom." Sam Fathers reenacts the doom of the Chickasaws, dying with Old Ben, and the wilderness itself is now subject to mortality. Faulkner, however, "declines to accept the end of man," and the Indian line is renewed in Ike, who must also bear the weight of southern history. At the end of Faulkner's great creative period, and in the last moment when the South, with all its faults, was still an entity, he combines the brotherhood of fallen man and the heroic vision of the hunt.[13]

One hesitates before adding to the criticism of "The Bear." One need not add to the allegorizing which Faulkner invites and under which, from the Nobel Prize till after his death, the story was buried. There are theories of why it is Boon who kills the bear, and with a knife, which make no mention of the frontier background. One

13. Francis Parkman, *Works,* Centenary Edition, 20 Vols. (New York, 1920), X, pp. ix–x.

can find the snake whom Ike greets as his grandfather, in the Indian way, simultaneously identified with "evil incarnate" and with old Carothers McCaslin. Even the major studies seem remote from the culture Faulkner writes about, as documented in the 1960s in the reminiscences of his brothers and his hunting friends.[14] No set of abstractions can be imposed upon the rhetoric of Part IV, where Rousseau and Keats, theology, the lost cause, and anticipations of the Nobel speech meet; where rank stereotypes of black incompetence are juxtaposed with the lived history of the ledgers, the marvelous humorous pathos of Mr. Hubert's silver cup, Ike's empty social heritage. Ike's gesture of relinquishment, one which, Michael Millgate points out, his creator took exception to, must be understood in its whole context.[15]

Interpretation of the tale has been subordinated in the recent interest in the unity and genetic development of *Go Down, Moses.* Disagreements about these subjects remain, but it can no longer be said that the revision of the separate stories was piecemeal or haphazard.[16] And

14. The exception is Brooks's *William Faulkner: The Yoknapatawpha Country* (New Haven and London, 1963), where "The Bear" is read within *Go Down, Moses* with a graceful sensibility and common sense. The local background of the tale is first fully acknowledged in the notes of James Early's study of the manuscripts, *The Making of Go Down, Moses* (Dallas, 1972).

15. Michael Millgate, *The Achievement of William Faulkner* (New York, 1963), 206.

16. This was the thesis of Marvin Klotz, "Procrustean Revision in Faulkner's *Go Down, Moses,*" *American Literature,* XXXVII (March, 1965), 1–16. Traces of his denial of the unity of the novel survive, paradoxically, in Early's view of the revisions, but from Millgate's pages in *The Achievement of William Faulkner* to Early's work, the studies of the texts, including an unpublished dissertation by Henry Ploegstra, "William Faulkner's *Go Down, Moses*: Its Sources, Revisions, and Structure" (University of Chicago, 1966), have revealed Faulkner's control of his material.

the others are less overshadowed by "The Bear." "Was" will be recognized as a classic, like "The Old People"; "The Fire and the Hearth" and "Pantaloon in Black" will be seen as valuable portraits of black character and culture. A substantial racial critique of *Go Down, Moses* may be expected, one which establishes that, as the black critic Sterling Brown says, "when he stands back and lets his Negro character speak out, and act out, Faulkner is right, and often superb." [17]

In the 1970s we can recognize that "The Bear" itself may be overwritten without minimizing its greatness. Faulkner expands his tall tale into a small-scale *Moby-Dick*, a frontiersman's *Paradise Lost*. His romanticism is sometimes disproportionate to its subject, as when Lion is carried back from the field like a dying hero, in a scene which both reasserts and parodies the traditions of chivalry and valor. The lack of perspective upon oneself is as southern as the belief that Gettysburg was one of the great battles of history. When he imitates Melville, Faulkner's tendency toward bombast is clear. "A whale-ship was my Harvard and my Yale College" becomes "the wilderness the old bear ran was his college and the old male bear itself, so long unwifed and childless as to have become its own ungendered progenitor, was his alma mater." Great writing always risks parodying itself as it approaches the limits of the possible. Faulkner, with his absolute standards, remarked that his generation would be judged by "the splendor of our failures," and his profound feeling for the wilderness as it both dwarfs and ennobles man sustains the splendor of the tale.

The Indian theme is an essential strand, from the

17. Sterling A. Brown, "A Century of Negro Portraiture in American Literature," *Massachusetts Review*, VII (Winter, 1966), 89–90.

opening affirmation of the Indian blood of Sam Fathers and Boon to Ike's visit to Sam's grave at the end. The hunt is an imitation of the frontier and Indian way of life, and Sam passes on to Ike the skills and values of the vanished Chickasaws. Beginning by finding the bear's footprint, at thirteen "he found a buck's bedding place by himself and . . . lay in wait for the buck at dawn and killed it when it came back to the bed as Sam had told him how the old Chickasaw fathers did." Under Sam's tutelage he becomes a mighty hunter. Behind them are old General Compson and Major de Spain, McCaslin Edmonds, and Walter Ewell, who return to the Big Bottom to feel like men in the image in which the wilderness created their forefathers. Here woodsmanship determines rank.

The hunting camp is Faulkner's continuity with Indian times, and it is an image of the ideal society, where everyone has his place and has something to do, a society which has its being in a purely natural setting and natural skills. The American belief in roughing it finds its apostle in the boy:

> He saw the camp—a paintless six-room bungalow set on piles above the spring high-water—and he knew already how it was going to look. He helped in the rapid orderly disorder of their establishment in it and even his motions were familiar to him, foreknown. Then for two weeks he ate the coarse, rapid food—the shapeless sour bread, the wild strange meat, venison and bear and turkey and coon which he had never tasted before—which men ate, cooked by men who were hunters first and cooks afterward; he slept in harsh sheetless blankets as hunters slept.

The passage shows the writer's pleasure in this discipline. "Sometimes the weather gets pretty rough, and sometimes the going gets hard," John Cullen says. "These are the things that prove what a man is made of. And William Faulkner has proved himself as good a man as ever went in the woods with us." [18]

Even in the woods, however, the hunters are of the society they leave behind. "Only Sam and Old Ben and the mongrel Lion were taintless and incorruptible," Faulkner says, reversing the southern cult of race and lineage. It is the tragic theme of a civilization burdened by original sin and a pure primitive life , and the Indians are not exempted from the corruption. Although Sam Fathers is "taintless," Ikkemotubbe was not. On the first page of the tale the chief is named among those who thought they owned the land—"white man fatuous enough to believe that he had bought any fragment of it," "Indian ruthless enough to pretend that any fragment of it had been his to convey." Ike begins his argument in Part IV with the violation of the tribal principle of communal landholding. Having learned from Sam that he cannot see the bear when "tainted" by watch and compass, he also tells his cousin that the land was "already tainted" before the white man took possession of it, by the Indians' acquisition of the white man's slaves.

One can assume that Faulkner, growing up on Cooper Indians, was disillusioned to find how readily red men in his part of the country had succumbed to what he saw as fatal evils of his own culture. But with his biblical grounding he was willing to believe that the sharers in the pure life of the wilderness would disregard its laws. He found support for this in the passage in which Rousseau laments the origin of property, which he had used in the chief's letter to the president in "Lo!":

18. Cullen and Watkins, *Old Times*, 12.

The first man, who, after enclosing a piece of ground, took it into his head to say, "This is mine", and found people simple enough to believe him, was the true founder of civil society. How many crimes, how many wars, how many murders, how many misfortunes and horrors, would that man have saved the human species, who pulling up the stakes or filling up the ditches, should have cried to his fellows: "Be sure not to listen to this imposter: you are lost, if you forget that the fruits of the earth belong equally to us all, and the earth itself to nobody!" [19]

Faulkner must have known this well, for it is also echoed in *The Unvanquished* and *Absalom, Absalom!* Buck and Buddy believed "that land did not belong to people but that people belonged to land," and where Thomas Sutpen grew up "the land belonged to anybody and everybody and so the man who would go to the trouble and work to fence off a piece of it and say 'This is mine' was crazy." [20] Here the writer is working out what he admired in the frontier democracy.

Ike sets Rousseau's vision of the fall of man in the biblical frame, with Ikkemotubbe as his Adam:

He created man to be His overseer on the earth and to hold suzerainty over the earth and the animals on it in his name, not to hold for himself and his descendants inviolable title forever, generation after generation, to the oblongs and squares of the earth, but to hold the earth mutual and intact in the communal anonymity of brotherhood . . . it was never Ikkemotubbe's father's fathers' to

19. Jean Jacques Rousseau, "Discourse on the Origins and Foundations of Inequality Among Men," *The First and Second Discourses*, ed. Roger O. Masters (New York, 1964), 141–42.

20. William Faulkner, *The Unvanquished* (New York, 1965), 54; William Faulkner, *Absalom, Absalom!* (New York, n.d.), 221. Melvin Backman first called attention to these parallels in *William Faulkner: The Major Years* (Bloomington, Ind., and London, 1966), 168.

bequeath Ikkemotubbe to sell to Grandfather or any man because on the instant when Ikkemotubbe discovered, realised, that he could sell it for money, on that instant it ceased ever to have been his forever, father to father to father, and the man who bought it bought nothing.

This closely resembles the southern Indians' conception of landholding, as established by a scholar who objects to some of Faulkner's emphases: "All of the Southeastern or 'civilized' tribes believed in communal holding. The land of the tribe belonged to all of the tribe but none of it exclusively to any one member of the tribe, except for a lifetime. Only the tribe, in the person of its chief, could sell the land. The chief, in turn, had it from the Great Spirit—as he had the tribe—for his appointed time. Only God owned either outright." The writer, M. E. Bradford, adds that "as late as 1897, Chief Dennis Bushyhead urged the Oklahoma Cherokees and neighboring tribes against any modern style private holding," and that "even now the oil-rich Tyonek Indians of Alaska persist, on religious grounds, in opting for tribal property." Bradford calls this feudal rather than communistic. Among the southern nations, he says, "one man, even an outsider, if favored by the tribe, did own a particular piece of land vis-à-vis another man: one more than any others." None of this arrangement was anonymous, and "tribal apportionment matched personal worth and need." [21]

Faulkner's essential point that the chief knew better than to sell the land remains valid, if we add that the Indians initially did not know what whites meant by buying it. They soon found out, as we saw in "Lo!"; and the record of their dispossession is full of accusations of be-

21. M. E. Bradford to author, March 26, 1973.

trayal, often by a majority of the full bloods, and of the annuities, the gifts of "money or rum or whatever it was," as Faulkner says, to which one chief or another responded. So in his old age in "The Bear" Ikkemotubbe casually betrays his heritage. In youth the nature's nobleman of "A Courtship" and *Requiem for a Nun*, then the tyrant of "A Justice," who makes the tribal land his personal domain, he is now saddled with the irreversible step which justifies the name of Doom.

To see Faulkner's break with nineteenth-century American thinking one must realize that what rationalized both the removal of the southern tribes and the restriction of the Indians to reservations under government control was above all their lack of a conception of private property. In the time of the religion of progress they were a remnant of man's savage state, to be duly converted from a hunting to a farming culture and to private land tenure. Roy Harvey Pearce quotes from a sympathizer with the Indians who, after surveying the history of their contacts with the whites, always resulting in Indian defeat and degradation, concludes that "the insecurity of property, or rather the entire absence of all ideas of property, is the chief cause of their barbarism." "The chain of causes by which the unhappy race must, if at all, be ameliorated will be this: first, personal security, by the entire abolition of war among them; secondly, permanent habitations, and thirdly, notions of property." [22] Faulkner's lack of illusions about bourgeois society or the improvement of human nature, as both a twentieth-century man and a southerner, kept him from thinking

22. James Hall, *Sketches of History, Life, and Manners in the West* (New York, 1835), I, 27–133, quoted in Roy Harvey Pearce, *The Savages Of America: A Study of the Indian and the Idea of Civilization* (Baltimore, 1953), 72.

in such terms, and he saw the Indian through his own love for the wilderness and the hunt. "As hunter he must die; as hunter he was dying," Pearce says. Unlike the nineteenth-century novelists, Faulkner takes this as an unmixed loss. He puts it in the context of the corruption of the new world, and identifies the dying Indian way of life with the best of his own society.

How, though, can he reconcile the redeeming virtues of the hunt with the Indians' collaboration in their own downfall? How can he reach back to the world already lost in the four stories of the Chickasaws and Choctaws? Sam Fathers' mixed blood is the answer. He is an Indian whose background of slavery exempts him from the guilt of the owners, whose repudiated black heritage counters the whitening of the southern tribes. Paradoxically, the curse from which Sam escapes into the wilderness and the Indian heritage makes him a "taintless" representative of this heritage in his creator's eyes. The red man is incorporated in a larger primeval past, one both historical and ontological. The confrontation of Indian and white becomes that of the land, the wilderness, the old people, versus a succession of men, Indians, whites, blacks —four, perhaps five, societies and races are enumerated in the Cass-Ike dialogue. The pervasive underlying conflict is one of immortality and time.

The Sam Fathers of "The Bear" is seen only within the wilderness and in an identification with its life which makes his authority complete. As the hunt is focused from the first on the looming figure of Old Ben, "phantom, epitome and apotheosis of the old wild life" which from the age of ten Ike calls his heritage, so Sam partakes of the bear's primacy. "Because he's the head bear. He's the man," Sam says, explaining how Ben comes every year to check out the hunters and their dogs. To the other hunters, as to the boy, Sam Fathers is really "the man," although General Compson is formally in charge. He is always ahead of them and they instinctively turn to him with a problem. To the boy he also represents the deeper meaning of the hunt, which the others cannot see.

The ritual of "The Bear" is a supremely eclectic product of Faulkner's experience, reading, and imagination. It was blacks who, in a southern childhood, humanized animals and their ways; and it is no accident that when Sam calls Old Ben "the man" who checks up on the hunters—"he do it every year"—he falls into black dialect. The Chickasaws themselves drew on black sources in weaving myths about their totem animals, according to the anthropologist Frank Speck.[23] However much Faulkner knew of this, the materials collected in *Bear, Man, and God* show his knowledge of bear ceremonialism among other North American tribes. Frazer was one source— there is a chapter in *The Golden Bough* on "Killing the Sacred Bear," which Faulkner momentarily echoes.[24] Thomas Bangs Thorpe's tale, "The Big Bear of Arkan-

23. Frank G. Speck, "Notes on Chickasaw Ethnology and Folk-Lore," *Journal of American Folk-Lore,* XX (January–March, 1907), 54.

24. "However, the men sometimes drink the warm blood of the bear 'that the courage and other virtues it possesses may pass into them,'" Frazer writes in *The Golden Bough,* p. 587, adding that "sometimes they besmear themselves and their clothes with the blood in order to ensure success in hunting." Faulkner transfers the virtues of the blood to the whiskey his hunters drink and modifies their motivation. "There was always a bottle present, so that it would seem to him that those fine fierce instants of heart and brain and courage and wiliness and speed were concentrated and distilled into that brown liquor which not women, not boys and children, but only hunters drank, drinking not of the blood they spilled but some condensation of the wild immortal spirit, drinking it moderately, humbly even, not with the pagan's base and baseless hope of acquiring thereby the virtues of cunning and strength and speed but in salute to them."

sas," brought all this into the context of frontier story-telling. Here was "an unhuntable bear who died when his time had come," with whom Thorpe's narrator identifies himself.

One finds elements of African religious symbolism in "The Bear" as well. The dominating presence of the forest and Sam Fathers' role as forest priest parallel West African cults which took root in the new world. "In the mind of the black man of Cuba," a scholar writes, "there persists an astonishingly tenacious belief in the spiritual force of the forest." [25] The leaves have both healing and magical powers, and these are controlled by Osanyin, lord of the leaves, tutelary spirit of the world of the Yoruba. He was also carried to Brazil—a comparative study in 1957 shows a photograph of a priest kneeling at the foot of a gigantic sacred tree—and influenced the conjurors of New Orleans and the Deep South. The initiate in the cult of Osanyin learns to read the forest word by word as a document—"bigger and older than any recorded document," Faulkner says—from the "babalawo," a priestly figure who, like Sam Fathers, is named as if he embodied all the priestly figures of his ancestors. The latter undergoes a ritual humiliation comparable to Sam Fathers' experience as a black in the South, from which Sam grows big again in the leaves and the wilderness.[26]

25. Lydia Cabrera, *El Monte* (Havana, 1954; reprinted Miami, Editions C. R., 1971); quoted by Robert Farris Thompson, "Aesthetic of the Cool: Towards a Transatlantic Study of African and Afro-American Art," a work in progress, to be published by Harper and Row, 55. Mr. Thompson, associate professor of African art at Yale, has allowed me to quote from his forthcoming book and has brought the other sources here and in the next paragraph to my attention. I am indebted to his understanding of the cult of Osanyin and its priest.

26. On Osanyin in Africa and the New World see Pierre Verger, *Notes sur le culte des Orisa et Vodin a Bahia, la Baie de tous les saintes, et a*

Robert Farris Thompson, who has pointed out these parallels to me, writes that the priest of Osanyin honors the forest, "teaching its impartial spirituality, teaching that the woods and birds are grander than any document, teaching that man cannot assume the earth is his alone, or else be answerable to God." [27] The "strong resonant African flavor" of "The Bear" suggests to him that Faulkner was exposed to a conjuror's lore, perhaps by the blacksmith himself. Indians did not work in iron, although the African blacksmith has artistic and spiritual functions, evidence of which have reappeared in the United States.[28] The survival of a god like Osanyin is a practical matter. One learns the leaves and the traditional verses which adorn their names to accomplish things—to get money, be protected from witches, get or recover a woman, be victorious over an enemy, enjoy a long life, get children and keep them alive. African symbolisms make mysteries of these mundanities. So in the hunting ritual a practical act becomes a sacramental communion.

Sam Fathers is scarcely a utilitarian figure, however. He sets Ike on a path which loses him his property, his wife, his chance of a posterity. Sam's Indian pride is distinguished from the endurance and strength Faulkner associates with the blacks. The fate of the American wilderness and theme of the vanishing red man intersect with Faulkner's Christian and Thoreauvian premises.

l'ancienne cotes des esclaves en Afrique (Dakar, 1957), 229–31. See also Verger's *Awon ewe Osanyin* [*The Leaves of Osanyin*] (Institute of African Studies, University of Ife, 1967), for the leaves and the verses which adorn their names and state their purposes.

27. Robert Farris Thompson, "Aesthetic of the Cool," 67.

28. Robert Farris Thompson, in conversation with the author, January 6 and 16, 1973.

Frazer's dying god is another influence, limiting the African parallel. Faulkner's priest dies with the bear, the manifestation of his god, after shaping the boy to the god's service. Sam knows that the great hunt is his doom. When brought in to interpret Lion's tracks, for example, he lets the hunters think it is a wolf, while Ike in retrospect sees foreknowledge in the old man's face. "It was almost over now and he was glad." The death of the bear will mean the end of the wilderness itself, the irremediable disappearance of a race and a civilization. Sam Fathers accepts the event as the inscrutable Indian of American folk myth, secret, impenetrable, and a fountainhead of knowledge.

Beside Sam and Old Ben in Faulkner's tableau are the great blue dog, Lion, calling forth memories of Paul Bunyan's blue ox Babe, and Boon Hogganbeck with his plebian strain of Indian blood. Faulkner is fond of Boon, with his harsh humor, his devotion to Lion, his loyalty to Ike and Sam. He is the grandson of David Hogganbeck, who eventually married a squaw of less note than Herman Basket's sister. He is to Sam Fathers as, in "The Fire and the Hearth," Zack Edmonds is to Lucas Beauchamp, the latter a generation closer to old Carothers and in the male line. Ike's romantic imagination makes Boon the huntsman of the Indian prince, and through him Faulkner arranges the "Greek gesture," as he called it, of Sam's death, and the savage funeral carried out with the boy's aid.

Boon being a quarter-Indian, we are entitled to suspect, by analogy with Sam Fathers, that his model was an eighth if that. He is partly drawn from Buster Callicot, the senior Falkner's stable foreman, with whom Faulkner told of having bought a Texas pony like those in "Spotted

Horses." [29] Ike recalls the episode when he gives Boon a dollar for a drink in Memphis. John Faulkner says his brother and Buster took the Memphis trip to buy whiskey for Stone's camp, and this comic interlude within the hunting scene is autobiographical in feeling.[30] Faulkner crossed his boyhood friend with two frontier figures, one the half-breed who violently denies his Indian blood except when violently asserting it (usually when drunk), the other the type of half-wild man who, according to John Cullen, used to hide out in the Big Bottom. The name Boon Hogganbeck reflects affectionate perspective. It suits the man's magnificence in the death scenes of Old Ben and Lion—with his love for the dog he can kill the bear with a knife not a gun, as Daniel Boone did it, as Faulkner wants it done—and his hysterical possessiveness at the squirrel tree in the last scene.

The central experience of the hunt is the boy's discovery that it must have an end. The "yearly pageant-rite of the old bear's furious immortality" is only immortal in Faulkner's work, like the lovers' pursuit on Keats's urn. At ten, as in "The Old People," Ike believes that "there would be a next time, after and after," and the Keatsian image is sustained when the bear appears to him the next year. He comes upon the fresh footprints, dissolving back into the swamp as he follows them:

29. Gwynn and Blotner (eds.), *Faulkner in the Univerity*, 29–30.
30. "This was the road over which Bill and Mr. Buster Callicot made the first and last part of their journey to Memphis for more whiskey (both incidents appear in "The Bear") when the camp supply ran out, and Mr. Buster got back with the partially wrapped corset he had bought as a present for his wife trailing under his arm." John Faulkner, *My Brother Bill*, 92. William Faulkner replaces the wife and corset with humorous details appropriate to Boon, who is another bachelor of nature.

Even as he looked up he saw the next one, and, moving, the one beyond it; moving, not hurrying, running, but merely keeping pace with them as they appeared before him as though they were being shaped out of thin air just one constant pace short of where he would lose them forever and be lost forever himself, tireless, eager, without doubt or dread, panting a little above the strong little hammer of his heart, emerging suddenly into a little glade and the wilderness coalesced.

Ike is "forever panting and forever young," the bear has the immortality of something that, as Faulkner said, will always move. No ordinary animal, it enters and leaves the clearing mysteriously, like the two deer in "The Old People," an emanation of life itself.

By thirteen, however, Ike can understand that there will be a last day. When even he [Old Ben] don't want it to last any longer." He and Sam have each refused a chance to shoot the bear, a refusal McCaslin interprets to him via Keats's ode. Lion's role is announced, and the dog's entry in Ike's fourth summer in camp transforms the "yearly rendezvous" into "the last act on a set stage." Lion's indomitable spirit sets off the deepening elegiac tone. The hunt becomes a preparation for death, the dramatic imagination of boyhood is played off against a new sense of what it means to be a man.

Faulkner's climax is prepared for and savored. "Weather gonter break today," old Ash says on the December morning of the Memphis trip in Ike's sixteenth year, and Boon seconds this that night, saying, "Lion will get him tomorrow." The chase in which "the gloomed woods rang and clamored" leads to the tableau of heroic death, with the three figures locked in each other's arms and falling like a tree, and Sam Fathers down in the mud behind them. The tone is sustained as Boon bleeds in the rain, "his face calm beneath the steady thinning of the bright blood," and the men return to camp "through the streaming and sightless dark," guided by spaced shots and the wailing hunting horn. Faulkner's echo of the *Chanson de Roland* becomes his "Goodnight, sweet prince" when Lion dies on the gallery at sundown the next day, facing the woods and all those who have come to see him and the body of his foe, to talk quietly "of hounds and bear and deer and men of yesterday vanished from the earth." Death is justified to our emotions in the epic mode.

The ritual leads to the death of the surrogate father, last of the Indians of Yoknapatawpha. "The old man, the wild man not even one generation from the woods, childless, kinless, peopleless," Sam Fathers reverts to the old tongue, preparing to go while the doctor says he will be fine. He is also the vanishing southerner, and his will to die has slavery behind it. "Let me out, master. Let me go home," he says as they take him back to camp. "Swing Low, Sweet Chariot" is joined to "Go Down, Moses," but there is no sentimentality for the reader who recalls that "for over seventy years now he had had to be a Negro. It was almost over now and he was glad."

Sam Fathers' death occurs offstage, with the implication—Faulkner was definite about it at Virginia—that Boon killed him at his request, like a great man's servant in the ancient world. The scene with the four posts and the blanket-wrapped bundle upon the platform and Boon and the boy squatting between the platform and the grave shows the power of the Indian legend for Faulkner, and for the American imagination. Faulkner's refer-

ence is not limited—a burial above ground, part of the
ancient Choctaw funeral, is also an African burial for a
chief. The loyalty and romanticism of childhood are his
vehicle. The boy and Boon, who "has the mind of a
child," keep the vision alive, in conflict with adult authority. When they are interrupted by McCaslin and
Major de Spain, Ike cuts off McCaslin's questioning of
Boon with the "leave him alone" which ends Part III of
"The Bear." It expresses the reader's exhaustion, like the
tears which spring from the boy's face like sweat, and is
a defense of the writer's imagined world.

The great days will not return, but the Indian background is sustained in Part IV in the contrast between the
wilderness and the "tamed land" as well as the argument
itself, Ike's renunciation and its reasoning. "Sam Fathers
set me free," he says. The echo of "Go Down, Moses" also
parallels Chief Joseph's statement that his father "wished
to be a free man. He claimed that no man owned any part
of the earth, and a man could not sell what he did not
own." [31] Part V, which opens with de Spain's selling off
the forest to progress, shows the actual transfer of the Indian heritage to Ike, who must live with his freedom in a
fallen world. The new age is exemplified by the planing
mill and miles of stacked rails and ties awaiting him at
Hoke's, and the logging train which "had been harmless
once." In the spirit of American pastoral it is compared to
a snake, anticipating the snake at Sam's grave; and old
Ash in the wagon warns that "they're crawling." The
memory of the old black's comic hunting accident has a
dual purpose, setting off Ike's maturity as a hunter even
as it evokes his own piety toward "the old man born of a

31. Chief Joseph, "An Indian's View of Indian Affairs," in Sanders and
Peek (eds.), *Literature of The American Indian*.

Negro slave and a Chickasaw chief who had been his spirit's father if any had," and toward the woods his mother and, he thinks, his future mistress and his wife."

The Indian theme is part of the "great prose hymn to nature," as Cleanth Brooks calls it, of Faulkner's conclusion. Like Cash the carpenter, he brings his planks into a final juxtaposition. The young woodsman out of Cooper knows his way to the knoll with its concrete markers, "lifeless and shockingly alien in that place where dissolution itself was a seething turmoil of ejaculation, tumescence, conception and birth, and death did not even exist." Ike's knife easily finds the can containing Old Ben's dried mutilated paw, resting above Lion's bones, and there is no need to look for Sam Fathers' grave somewhere beneath his feet—" 'He probably knew I was in the woods this morning long before I got here,' he thought." The animate universe takes the place of orthodox faith in the traditional elegy.

Faulkner's eclecticism gives us the Indian buried with hunting horn, knife, and pipe, and the white youth replenishing the tobacco as in a Greek libation rite, leaving at the grave also "the small paper sack of the peppermint candy Sam had used to love." Tobacco and candy are Zack Edmonds' gifts to old Molly Beauchamp, who is modeled on Faulkner's mammy, Callie Barr. Ike's offerings are immediately absorbed into "the myriad life which printed the dark mold of these secret places with delicate fairy tracks"; and the mysterious process and presence evoke the vision of Lion and Sam "not held fast in earth but free in earth and not in earth but of earth," a majestic Whitmanesque affirmation which goes back to the young Faulkner's assertion in verse, "Though I be dead, / This earth that holds me fast will find me breath." It may also owe something to the old Indian mounds, and is followed by a Keatsian image of the happy hunting ground, with the prey brought back to life after the promise of "The Old People," "Then the long challenge and the long chase, no heart to be driven and outraged, no flesh to be mauled and bled"—the dream is broken off as Ike freezes to the rattler at his knee.

Precise description guarantees the symbolic force of this great moment. The way Ike takes his weight on one foot and controls his fear, the look of the old snake, "one loop cast sideways as though merely for purchase from which the raised head might start slightly backward, not in fright either, not in threat quite yet," support the invocation of "the old one, the ancient and accursed about the earth," with the smell "evocative of all knowledge and an old weariness and of pariah-hood and of death." "The snake is the old grandfather, the old fallen angel, the unregenerate immortal," as Faulkner said at Virginia, adding that "the good and shining angel ain't very interesting." [32] The American wilderness has become a paradise lost where woodsmanship and courage are conditions of survival. Ike knows he has been fully accepted by the wilderness when the snake does not strike him, and it is natural for him to salute its departing shape, as he puts his other foot down at last, in the words Sam had used with the great deer. " 'Chief,' he said. 'Grandfather.' "

The totem greeting does not mean what it does in "The Old People," where the priest celebrates both his own race and universal life. Nor is it the simpler ac-

32. Gwynn and Blotner (eds.), *Faulkner in the University*, 2.

knowledgment of the principle of life and death in "Red Leaves." Ike accepts his place in the world of men doomed not only to die, but to cut down the woods which are their glimpse of immortality. He simultaneously subordinates the Christian symbolism to the communion of the forest and reaffirms his faith in the wilderness god. Natural and ancestral piety are joined. His grandfather lives, though his "spirit's father" is gone, and he can take Sam's place and preserve the ritual.

The continuity with "Red Leaves" and "The Old People" is that in these words a man of another race *becomes* an Indian, keeping the heritage alive. Whatever the source of the national belief in the Vanishing American's return, Faulkner held to and reinforced it in the eclipse of the southern tribes. The literary man's material was the moralist's alternative to the plantation and to mechanized modernity. Blacks and whites purified by the Indian culture and meeting on this ground—this is Faulkner's romantic melting-pot mythology.

His historical pessimism returns in the closing vignette of Boon beneath the tree full of squirrels, wildly beating at his jammed gun and crying out, "Don't touch a one of them! They're mine!" The survivor of the hunt, the last man of Indian blood, is reduced to petty comedy and returns us to the curse of property and possession. Faulkner took the episode and the cry, "They're mine!" from a hunting experience of which he liked to tell, involving a man named Westmoreland who had a rickety, single-barrel shotgun pieced together with baling wire.[33] In "The Bear" it becomes much more than buffoonery,

33. Bramlett Roberts retells Faulkner's story, in Webb and Green (eds.), *William Faulkner of Oxford*, 151–52: "Bill heard some shooting over in a clearing and when he got in sight he saw a large oak tree with no other trees around it and the squirrels were playing all over the tree. Wes had shot his gun. When it fired the barrel came off: the stock went

more even than the Rousseauist moral. As Brooks says, Boon sees the end of the wilderness in the lumber company's work, the background of his hysteria. "He lacks Isaac's lettered sensibility and spiritual resources, but Boon, too, senses that the old world has been lost, and in a kind of desperation he would hold onto—would frantically fend others away from—the tree full of squirrels which represents something of the abundance and freedom of the old wilderness." [34] In this sense he too is transfigured by his experience, frustrated and doomed as, in their nobler ways, are Sam and Ike.

This is the end of the story which began with the Indians of "Lo!" making the whites play their own game and with Ikkemotubbe and David Hogganbeck "looking at" the same woman. It is a fragmentary story—all beginning and ending, in fact—and told in different styles matched to the author's changing interests. The continuity through Sam Fathers need not be pressed. But one can see how Faulkner first imagined the world of which the old man spoke and then made him and the young listener its heirs. The historical vision is cyclical. The vigor of "Lo!" and innocence of "A Courtship" give way to the decay of "Red Leaves," from which the heroic hunting mythology emerges, to ripen with "The Bear" and fade with the wilderness itself in "Delta Autumn." Like the Indian stories, *Go Down, Moses* moves from a lost world of "was" to the world in which we live.

And what are these tales worth in our world, extravagant as they are, remote as they may seem from the ethnic politics and writing of the American 1970s? One hopes

---

one way, the barrel another, and the forearm another. Bill went up and was going to kill some of the squirrels; it was full of squirrels. And Wes said, 'Oh no, don't bother 'em. They're mine!'" Mr. Roberts had not apparently then read "The Bear."

34. Brooks, *The Yoknapatawpha Country*, 271.

this book will have suggested a few preliminary answers. "It has become fashionable today," as Jerome Rothenberg writes in *Shaking the Pumpkin*, "to deny the possibility of crossing the boundaries that separate people of different races and cultures; to insist that black is the concern of black, red of red, and white of white." [35] That the archetypal southern novelist should so successfully challenge these boundaries is an irony of history comparable only to Lyndon Johnson singing "We Shall Overcome" —not, indeed, synthetic, as some found President Johnson synthetic, but expressing the same victory of experience and imagination over doctrine. Faulkner writes of Indians and blacks as reflectors of his own culture, of its history and feeling, of course, but he also energetically works against its limitations.

"The Bear" has already had an influence across racial boundaries. A hunter's initiation in N. Scott Momaday's *House Made of Dawn*, published separately as "The Bear and the Colt," depends on Faulkner's rhythm and his rhetoric. Evoking the animate universe, "brooding . . . ancient and inviolable," Momaday dwells on an image of the bear in perfect phase with the hunter, "unhurried, certain of where it was and where he was and of every step of the way between, keeping always and barely out of sight, almost out of hearing." The hunter is in turn described "not hurrying but going only as fast as the bear had gone, going even in the bear's tracks, across the ravine and up the embankment and through the trees, unwary now, sensible only of closing in, going on and looking down at the tracks." This goes back to Ike following Old Ben's footsteps in the swamp, "not hurrying, run-

35. Jerome Rothenberg, *Shaking the Pumpkin: Traditional Poetry of the Indian North Americas* (Garden City, N.Y., 1972), xix.

ning, but merely keeping pace with them as they appeared before him . . . tireless, eager, without doubt or dread." There are other echoes, including the statement, after the bear's death, that "he [the youth] and the colt had come of age and were hunters too, now." [36] Faulkner had shaped the Indian writer's vision of the ritual of his people. The supreme irony is that the image of hunter and hunted to which he most strongly responds in turn reflects Faulkner's response to Keats.

Momaday, himself part Cherokee, may not be representative of less educated Indian writers, but the example suggests that the brotherhood of literature is stronger than the divisions of politics. There are consciously nationalistic Indians who are strongly influenced by the writings of white people. Others, of course, are not. There are tribes like the Navahos, Hopis, Sioux, with a strong continuity of tribal culture, but for the younger Indians in cities this is not the case. Leslie Fiedler has said that "today the Indian proceeds to reinvent himself—in part out of the mythology and science created by White people to explain him to themselves." [37] If this generalization contains as much truth as Fiedler's sometimes do, Faulkner's tales will have their influence. At any rate they show again the kind of regenerative insight and perspective provided by a major writer. They show how literature renews itself and is nourished by the land, how experience and local history, folk humor and romance, are catalysts of imaginative freedom and power.

36. N. Scott Momaday, *House Made of Dawn* (New York, 1967), 198–204, reprinted as "The Bear and the Colt," in Natachee Scott Momaday (ed.), *American Indian Authors* (Boston, 1972), 119–24.

37. Leslie A. Fiedler, *The Return of the Vanishing American* (New York, 1968), 12.

ᕫ Index

Absalom, Absalom!, 81, 103, 140
Adventures of Huckleberry Finn,
  The, 120–21
American Humor. See Rourke,
  Constance
American Indian Reader, 17–18
Animism. *See* Ritual; *Go Down,*
  Moses
As I Lay Dying, 88

Barr, Callie, 22, 25, 118, 152
Basket family: Herman Basket, 13,
  32–33, 78; "Herman Basket's sis-
  ter," 13, 57, 59, 61–62, 68, 70;
  Three Basket, 13, 90, 92, 99–101,
  107
"Bear Hunt, A," 19–21
"Bear, The," 4, 5, 11, 16, 23, 26, 39,
  41, 47–48, 54–57, 64, 84, 86, 88–89,
  110, 118–23, 128–29, 134; 135–57.
  See also Indian stories
"Bear, The": *Saturday Evening*
  Post version of, 121
Beauchamp, Lucas, 19, 65–66, 116,
  124, 147
Benson, Henry C., 10 *n*
Berry, Louis, 24, 90, 99–101, 105
Bibb, Henry, 84–85
Black Elk, 17 *n*
Blacks:
  —endurance of (theme): 16; in
  "Red Leaves," 74–76, 79, 82–83,
  90–92, 99–100, 110, 112, 116; in
  Go Down, Moses, 146
  —Indian ancestry: 9–10, 26–32,
  124; Faulkner's use of, 10, 15,
  26–32, 86–87, 104, 123–25. *See*
  also Ritual
Bradford, M. E., 55, 141
Brooks, Cleanth, 136 *n*, 152, 155
Brown, Calvin S., 11, 20 *n*, 23, 41 *n*,
  66, 67, 88, 109
Brown, Sterling A., quoted, 29, 37
Byrd, William, 18 *n*
Byron, Lord, 61

Cambon, Glauco, 131–32
Carolina Sports by Land and Wa-
  ter, 126–27
Cash, W. J., 64
Cherokees, 5–7, 9, 52, 58–59, 84, 86,
  116, 141, 157. *See also* Indians;
  Five Civilized Tribes
Chickasaws: traces of, in Lafayette
  County, 19–21, 24, 25–26; and
  Mississippi history, 34–35, 37;
  courtship of, 61–62; status of
  women among, 70, 77–78; decay
  of, 95–96; as slaveholders, 8–10
  86, 93–94, 96, 103; use of black
  mythology, 144; mentioned, 3, 5,
  7–8, 104. *See also* Indians; Five
  Civilized Tribes
Choctaws: remnant in Mississippi,
  7, 25–26, 29–31; and Mississippi

history, 34–35, 37, 46; as slave-holders, 9–10, 85–86, 124; burial among, 31, 151; mentioned, 3, 5, 7–8, 47 *n. See also* Indians; Five Civilized Tribes

Christmas, Joe, 67, 108

Cochise, Chief, 17

Collected Stories of William Faulkner, 3, 5 *n*

Commission to Five Civilized Tribes, Eleventh Annual Report to the Secretary of the Interior, 29–30

Compson, Quentin, 15, 18, 29, 72, 86, 89, 121

Conrad, Joseph, 106, 131

Cooper, James Fenimore, 22–23, 118, 120–21, 139, 152

"Courtship, A," 3–5, 11, 13–15, 23, 37–38, 42, 57–71, 75, 77, 80, 82–83, 89, 101, 103, 142, 155. *See also* Indian stories

Cowley, Malcolm: Faulkner's letters to, 12–14, 32, 76–77; mentioned, 5

Craw-ford (pappy), 75, 78–79, 80, 82

Creeks, 5–7, 9–10, 47 *n*, 51–52, 85–86. *See also* Indians; Five Civilized Tribes

Crèvecoeur, Hector St. John de, 38, 51

Cullen, John 120, 138–39, 148

Debo, Angie, 8 *n*, 25 *n*, 30, 78 *n*

Delany, Martin R., 85–86

Deloria, Vine, 17, 27 *n*

Dilsey, 23, 100, 116

Divine Comedy, 111, 121

Doom. *See* Ikkemotubbe

"Dry September," 91–92, 98

Edmonds, McCaslin, 121, 123, 128, 130, 133–35, 138, 149

Falkner, Murry C., 22, 24–25, 27–28

Fathers, Sam: Mississippi back-ground of, 25–33; in "A Justice," 4, 10, 14, 18, 26, 28–32, 72–76, 78, 86–89; in *Go Down, Moses*, 4, 15–16, 21–23, 29–32, 39, 41–42, 118–57 *passim*; as Indian and black, 14–15, 17, 39, 74–75, 86–87, 123–27, 135, 138, 143, 145, 150, 152. *See also* Noble savage; Vanishing American

Faulkner, John, 22, 28–29, 70, 73, 81, 119, 123, 148 *n*

Faulkner, William:
—as Darwinian: *See* Blacks, endurance of; Nobel Prize speech
—Frontier heritage, 3–4, 15–16, 22–23, 24 *n*, 33–34, 44–45, 48, 56, 57–66, 80–81, 118–20, 122–23, 125–27, 130–31, 135–40, 147–48, 152–55
—interviews and commentary: 6, 10–11, 12–13, 14, 21, 23, 32, 33, 41, 76–77, 81 *n*, 91, 100, 110, 115, 119, 128, 137, 153. *See also* Nobel Prize speech
—treatment of history: 8, 14, 16, 19–20, 24, 34; in "Lo!" 36, 43–56 *passim*; "A Courtship," 37, 58–59, 71; in "A Justice," 4, 8–10, 12, 29, 77–78, 84–86; in "Red Leaves," 4, 8–10, 12, 24, 35, 93–104, 111; in *Go Down, Moses*, 16–17, 29, 31, 37. *See also* Storytelling
—treatment of race: 18, 26, 36, 41, 156; in "Lo!" 49, 52, 71; in "A Courtship," 13, 57–60, 64, 66, 71, 83; in "A Justice," 4, 10, 14–15, 25–33, 72, 74–76, 80, 82–83, 85–87; in "Red Leaves," 90–91, 99–100, 103, 108–10, 115–17; in *Go Down, Moses*, 4, 15–16, 21–22, 25–32, 39, 120–21, 123–25, 129, 136–37, 139, 143, 152, 154
—use of life: 20–21, 24–25; in "A Courtship," 23, 61, 66, 70; in "A Justice," 28–29, 32–33, 72–75, 77; in "Red Leaves," 23, 109; in *Go Down, Moses*, 22–23, 28–29, 32–

33, 119–20, 123, 138–39, 147–48, 152, 154–55
Fiedler, Leslie A., 21, 59–60, 66, 71, 157
"Fire and the Hearth, The," 64, 72, 137, 142
Five Civilized Tribes, 5–6, 8–9, 30, 124, 141–42. *See also* Indians; Cherokees; Chickasaws; Choctaws; Creeks, Seminoles
Franklin, Benjamin, 49
Frazer, James G. See *Golden Bough, The*
Friedenberg, Edgar Z., 86

Genovese, Eugene D., 116
Gibson, Arrell, M., 8 *n*, 78 *n* 93–95, 103–104
Go Down, Moses, 4, 13–16, 25, 31–32, 41, 72, 76, 82, 117; 118–57. *See also* Indian stories
Gohdes, Clarence, 125
Golden Bough, The, 97–98, 107, 144 *n*, 147
"Grandfather (Compson)," 74, 78, 87, 89
Grayson, Mary, 85

Had-Two-Fathers, 32, 74, 83. *See also* Fathers, Sam
Hallowell, A. Irving, 38, 94
Hamlet, The, 50, 69–70, 89
Heart of Darkness, 131
Hemingway, Ernest, 11, 67, 101–102
Hogganbeck, Boon, 15, 30, 64, 119–21, 123, 130, 135, 138, 147–48, 151, 154–55
Hogganbeck, David, 57, 59–60, 62–69, 155
Holt, Minnie Smith, 12 *n*, 96
Houston, Sam, 58–59
Howe, Irving, 91
Howell, Elmo, 11–12, 31, 59–60, 76 *n*, 91, 93
Hughes, Langston, 27
Humor. *See* Indian stories

"If there be grief" (*A Green Bough*), 73, 152
Ikkemotubbe (Doom): in "A Courtship," 13, 15, 37, 57–71; in "A Justice," 13, 15, 24, 26, 32–33, 72–89; in *Go Down, Moses*, 15–16, 31–32, 47, 77, 117, 122, 139–42; mentioned, 21, 102, 105
Indians:
  —communal holding: 16, 48, 139–42, 151; in Faulkner, 15–16, 48, 54, 140. *See also* Rousseau
  —"progress" and assimilation: 5–6, 94; Indian resistance to, 16–17; Faulkner's view of, 38–39, in "Red Leaves," 90–117; and nineteenth-century view, 142–43
  —as slaveholders: 8–10, 12, 84–86, 93–96, 103; in "A Justice," 10, 72–89; in "Red Leaves," 10–11, 13, 90–117; in *Go Down, Moses*, 16, 55, 124–25
Indian stories: as chronicle, 3–5, 13–14, 42, 155; genealogy in, 13–15, 26, 32–33, 36, 64, 74–75, 78, 86, 102, 104, 123–24, 147; humor in, 3–4, 11, 17–18, 23–24; in "Lo!" 43–56; in "A Courtship," 60–61, 65, 68; in "A Justice," 72, 75, 78–79, 81–83; in "Red Leaves," 91–93, 98, 103–104, 111–12; in *Go Down, Moses*, 147–48, 151
Issetibbeha, 14 *n*, 61, 90, 93–94, 96, 101, 104–105

Jackson, Andrew, 6–7, 13, 35–36, 38, 45–46, 50, 53, 60, 65
Jefferson, Thomas, 18 *n*
Jeltz, Wyatt F., 9, 86, 94 *n*
Jobaker, 129–30
Joseph, Chief, 117, 151
"Justice, A," 3–5, 10–15, 18, 24, 26, 28–29, 31–32, 39–40, 57, 66, 71, 72–89, 98, 101, 103, 118, 124, 129, 134, 142; manuscript of, 32, 74, 77 *n*, 88. *See also* Indian stories

Kazin, Alfred, 91, 105

Lafferty, R. A., 9–10, 86
Last of the Mohicans, The, 22–23
LeFlore, Chief, 35–37, 45, 51, 53
Life against death (theme), in "Red
    Leaves," 106–15; in "The Bear,"
    147–50, 152–53
Light in August, 108
Linder, Felix, 115
"Lion," 121
"Lo!" 3–5, 13–14, 35–36, 42, 43–56;
    57–58, 60, 71, 139, 141, 155. *See
    also* Indian stories
Log-in-the-Creek, 57, 62, 69, 71
Lord Jim, 106

McCaslin, Carothers, 66, 77, 124,
    136
McCaslin, Isaac: as heir of Indians,
    4, 17, 22, 54–55, 117, 128–29, 131,
    133, 135, 151, 153–54; mentioned,
    13, 15–18, 22, 31, 54, 74, 89, 118–
    57 *passim*
"The Man," 36, 76, 83, 101, 105,
    106, 143–44
Manfred, Frederick, 97 *n*
Marlowe, Christopher, 81
Millgate, Michael, 136
Miner, Ward L., 12 *n*, 51 *n*, 70 *n*
*Mississippi, as a Province, Terri-
    tory, and State*, 37 *n*, 47, 61
*Mississippi Historical Society, Pub-
    lications of the*, 45, 61–62
Mississippi Territorial Archives,
    37, 46, 52
Moby-Dick, 22, 107, 118, 120–21,
    130, 137
Mohataha, 21, 34
Moketubbe, 90, 94, 96, 101, 104–
    107, 110–12, 117
Momaday, N. Scott, 156
"Mountain Victory," 35–36
Myrdal, Gunnar, 10, 103

Natchez, 7, 35, 96–97
"Negro, the," 90–94, 98–100, 106–17
Nilon, Charles H., 91
Nobel Prize speech, 66, 93, 99, 135–
    36

Noble savage, 4, 11, 15, 58, 104, 117,
    118, 124. *See also* Fathers, Sam,
    in *Go Down, Moses*

"Ode on a Grecian Urn," 89, 129,
    148, 153, 157
"Old People, The": *Harper's* ver-
    sion of, 121; manuscript of,
    134 *n*, mentioned, 4, 16, 18, 23,
    26, 28–29, 32, 41, 74, 86, 88, 110,
    118; 122–35; 137, 148–49, 153–54.
    See also Indian stories
"Oleh (Olé), Grandfather," 4, 16,
    39–41, 110, 129–30, 153. *See also*
    Ritual
Oral tradition. *See* Storytelling
Osanyin, cult of, 145–46

"Pantaloon in Black," 72, 137
Parkman, Francis, 135
Pearce, Roy Harvey, 11 *n*, 142–43
Pope, Alexander, 44, 50, 59
Porter, Kenneth W., 8, 10 *n*, 26–27,
    93
"President, the," 43–44, 47–50, 52–
    55
Pushmataha, Chief, 51, 53 *n*

"Red Leaves": manuscript of, 24,
    98 *n*; mentioned, 3–5, 10–11, 13–
    14, 23–24, 28, 34–35, 39–41, 57,
    66, 71, 72, 75, 77, 82–83, 86, 89,
    90–117; 134–35, 154–55. *See also*
    Indian stories
Requiem for a Nun, 5, 13, 21, 34
Ritual: African, 39–40, 110–11, 132,
    145–46, 151; Indian, 40–41, 96–
    97, 144; in southern hunt, 126–
    27; in Faulkner, 4, 16, 39–41,
    90–91, 94–95, 98–99, 107, 110–11,
    116–17, 126–35, 144–54. *See also
    Golden Bough*
Rourke, Constance, 33, 48, 63, 80
Rousseau, Jean Jacques, 16, 54–55,
    136, 139–40, 155. *See also* In-
    dians, communal holding

Sartoris, Bayard, 36

Satanta, Chief, 17
Seattle, Chief, 17
Seminoles, 5–6, 9–10. *See also* Indians; Five Civilized Tribes
Shaking the Pumpkin (Rothenberg), 156
Shorter, Frank, 108–109
Silverberg, Robert, 20 *n*, 97
Simms, William Gilmore, 43
Slavery. *See* Indians, as slaveholders
Sound and the Fury, The: appendix to, 21, 26, 76; manuscript of, 87; mentioned 28–29, 72–73, 87–88
Story-telling and Faulkner's tales, 17–18, 22, 24–25, 29, 32, 41–42, 72–73, 76, 88, 120, 132
Styron, William, 102
Sutpen, Thomas, 77, 81, 103, 124, 140

Tate, Allen, 55–56

Tecumseh, Chief, 140
"That Evening Sun," 73, 89
Thompson, Robert Farris, 145–46
Tocqueville, Alexis de, 7 *n*, 51, 69
Totemism. *See* Ritual; "Red Leaves"; *Go Down, Moses*

Unvanquished, The, 64, 140

Van Every, Dale, 6 *n*, 45, 58–59
Vanishing American, 4, 21–22, 135, 146, 154. *See also* Fathers, Sam, in *Go Down, Moses*
Vidal (Weddel), Francis, 47–48, 50–52, 54

Weddel, Saucier, 36
Wild Palms, The, 110 *n*

Yoknapatawpha, 4, 16, 22, 24, 39, 46, 77, 81, 130, 150
Yoruba, 40 *n*, 133 *n*, 145